Saved By A Blonde & A Chicken Pot Pie

A Restaurateur's Memoir

Bob Spivak

ISBN: 978-1-916954-19-9

Dedication

This book is for:
My parents, Lois Ames and Eddie Spivak,
for their work ethic and unwavering support,
the people who mentored me along the way,
my children, Jason and Elissa,
my step-children, Todd and Dayna,
my daughter-in-law Laurie Spivak for the initial push,
and for my wife, Leslie, without whom this book would not
have been possible.

Table of Contents

The Restaurant Business:
An Insider's View

Recipes

Acknowledgements

Restaurants aren't built by one person alone—they are a living, breathing reflection of the people and personalities that share the space, even if only for the duration of a meal.

We were fortunate that our restaurant(s) attracted movie and television stars, talent agents and Hollywood business powerbrokers, along with everyday guests, creating a blend of personalities that provided daily dramas worthy of their own television shows.

While I share selected stories about some of the various Hollywood personalities who passed through our doors, this book was never meant to be a "tell-all" Hollywood tale. Others may have their own recollections; this book is about my life, from my perspective.

Laurie Spivak, my daughter-in-law, researched and wrote several chapters on the history of my family's restaurants and The Grill on the Alley several years ago before I was able to fully commit to the undertaking of writing a book, and much of what she wrote is included in these pages.

I want to thank Laurie for her work and contributions, Thekla Fagerlie-Madsen for helping me put it all together, Marylouise Oates for the title, and of course, the "blonde," my wife Leslie, for her unwavering love and support.

Foreword

There is a time in your life when special people enter. One of those times for me was 1994. As President of an airport restaurant company at the time, I had the vision of changing the dining landscape at America's airports. The LAX concessions program was in bidding process; we made it 'ground zero' for bringing local concepts into the airport restaurant scene. That's when Bob Spivak and I met.

Bob was the renowned co-creator of The Grill on the Alley and creator of The Daily Grill. I was just a guy with a plan. Nervous as hell, I outlined my plan for LAX, hopeful that the Daily Grill would lead the bid. Bob paused, asked for more substance around the plan, pondered overnight, and was on board the next day. He saw something in me...and believed! Eventually, against all odds, we won the bid with the Daily Grill at Bradley terminal becoming one of finest airport restaurants in the world.

Bob had the respect of his restaurant peers who aligned with us in the process. It was amazing to watch. I asked several of them why they joined our bid. The overwhelming response was, "We trust that Bob will do the right thing, the right way." The strength of his character was evident.

My career continued to move on to new opportunities, but the relationship with Bob grew into one of the strongest friendships in my life. Not because we won the bid, but because Bob and I forged a bond of trust and honesty that began in 1994 and continues to this day, and includes Leslie and my wife, Sharon, who became great friends along the way.

Bob's values...humility, character, and integrity, all define him. His devotion to family drives him. Bob's life experiences are worth reading and absorbing. These learnings will give confidence and hope to others who begin their journey with obstacles in the way. His courage and perseverance to overcome his obstacles should resonate with any reader.

I have had the great pleasure to watch the care and concern he gives to his family, restaurant teams, and peers alike. I have been honored to hear the great stories of his life and be part of his life since our first encounter.

Bob is a good, good man...my great friend.

--Jon (Jack) Luther Chairman/CEO Dunkin' Brands, retired

My Life

Prologue

The Grill on the Alley - Opening Day
Beverly Hills, California – January 31, 1984

At precisely 11 a.m. I walked across the black-and-white checked marble floor, past the white linen-covered tables and green leather booths, took a deep breath, and unlocked the mahogany-framed glass doors that opened out to Dayton Way, a narrow alley off Wilshire Boulevard, one block away from Beverly Hills' famed Rodeo Drive. In a moment of panic, I worried that maybe the alley location had been a terrible idea and no one would be able to find us, so I carried a bar chair out to the sidewalk and propped a Now Open sign on the seat. My two partners, Michael Weinstock and Richard Shapiro, would not have agreed with the sign but that's how anxious I was. *This was it.* All the months of planning, building, hiring, ordering, arranging, and agonizing were over. The Grill on the Alley was open.

I wish I could claim that I knew The Grill on the Alley would be successful: that we had perfectly plotted our location down the street from Hollywood's biggest talent agencies; that our timing magically synchronized with a decade known for excess discretionary wealth; that our curated menu of classic meals and comfort foods would be embraced by our guests—famous and ordinary—and culinary professionals alike. The truth is, I didn't know any of this when we opened our doors on that last Tuesday in January 1984; an opening that almost didn't happen.

I was 38 years old, had struggled with learning disabilities all my life, and while I had grown up in the restaurant business and managed restaurants before, I never had a restaurant I could call my own—until now. The partnership that Michael, Richard, and I formed made it possible.

My ambitions were modest—I just needed a solid hit to regain my footing from some personal and financial challenges that had dogged me for several years. Hopefully, The Grill would be profitable enough so I could support my family and pay back our investors, many of whom were family and friends. I never imagined it would be a home run, much less a grand slam. None of us involved in this venture did.

The Grill on the Alley became a go-to lunch destination for Hollywood's dealmakers: studio heads, agents, managers, entertainment attorneys, producers, directors, and A-list celebrities of all types, as well as tourists and local residents; all were likely to cross paths at The Grill.

Over the years, The Grill has been many things to many people: a place to see and be seen, a place to do business, a place to celebrate, a place that felt like home in the chaotic, charismatic city of Los Angeles.

To me, The Grill was the sum of everything I had learned about food, the restaurant business, and about people. And although I didn't know it at the time, The Grill was also the launching point for future business ventures and my life with Leslie.

The path to success wasn't straight or easy, but it was well worth the journey.

This is my story.

Chapter 1
Food: It's in Our Genes

Food was the foundation of our family. In 1910, my grandfather, David Spivak, emigrated from the Ukraine to the United States and landed in Philadelphia. He sold apples as a street vendor and saved enough money to open a candy store on Walnut Street where he and my grandmother, Gussie, lived above the shop with their son Samuel E., known as "Eddie" (my father), and daughter Anna.

My dad used to tell a story about a huge pyramid of chocolates on the front counter of Papa David's shop. As a child, my father would take a chocolate out of the middle, eat half of it, and then turn it around and hide it in the middle of the stack; a six-year-old's version of a pyramid scheme.

The family moved to Los Angeles in 1929 and lived in Boyle Heights, which back then was home to a large Jewish immigrant community. My father went to Polytechnic High School in Boyle Heights and my mother, Lois, went to Los Angeles High School in the upper middle-class area of LA. They were introduced by mutual friends and married in 1937. It was an unusual match as they were from very different socioeconomic areas of the city with very different upbringings. My father never graduated from high school my mother went to college at the University of California-Los Angeles. My mother's family was also involved in the food industry, but on the supply side; my mother's Uncle Max owned a meatpacking business in Vernon, California.

Lois and Eddie Spivak, 1945

I came along one warm July day in 1943 during World War II. At this time, my father worked at Uncle Max's meatpacking house. As the food business was considered a necessary civilian occupation and food shortages were a critical problem during the war, food industry employees were exempted from military service.

I'm not sure what it says about how Uncle Max felt about his new nephew-by-marriage but he put my dad to work on the killing floor. One day toward the end of the war, a bull came through the kill chute. The chute was built to accommodate 1,500-pound animals, not the 2,000-pound brute that filled the space. My father hit the bull over the head with a wooden mallet, which didn't do the job. The bull, now incensed, broke through the chute and charged. My father ducked behind a brick wall that had been built for such an occasion. The bull rammed the wall, knocked it down, and died. That was my father's last day at the packing house. He decided that, like his own father, he would rather work with the end-user; it was far less gory and much safer.

Dad's first restaurant venture was a hamburger and hotdog stand called the Blue Diamond Grill located on Broadway. During World War II the Blue Diamond Grill became popular with GIs on leave who had no place to stay. They would walk up and down the streets of downtown Los Angeles into the early hours of the morning and buy hotdogs and hamburgers from my father. Soon, he had three Blue Diamond Grill hamburger stands all along Broadway. He recalled he probably made more money from these stands than at any other time in his life.

When the war ended, my father wanted to get into the conventional restaurant business, so he bought a coffee shop on the southeast corner of First and Broadway. Shortly after buying the coffee shop, the space next door became available. He took over the new space and opened the Redwood House in 1947, a place that would become significant to me a little later in my life. He was afraid to close the Blue Diamond Grill for fear someone else would take it over and compete with the Redwood House, but closed it five years later when the Redwood was firmly entrenched in the neighborhood.

After World War II ended, a housing boom started. The only lumber available for building the restaurant was Redwood, hence the name the Redwood House. Sharing a common wall with the *Los Angeles Times* building, the restaurant and bar quickly became the preferred watering hole of the Times reporters who considered the Red Dog, as they liked to call it, their "home away from home," much to the chagrin of their wives. It was both famous and infamous. Journalists celebrated winning Pulitzer Prizes at the Redwood. Newspapermen would bring their Olivetti typewriters, set them up at the bar, and type up their stories—using the hunt and peck method—while having a Manhattan...or two...or three. The wives would come in around 8 p.m. and drag their husbands home.

If a reporter was lucky enough to have his office on the

second floor above the bar, he could just stomp on the floor three times and a Manhattan would be waiting for him when he came down to the bar. There was also a direct line from the newspaper's switchboard to the bar: extension 1200.

Editors would call down looking for a reporter, and the red phone behind the bar would ring. It was a familiar dance and the bartender was a willing partner. It went something like this:

"I'm looking for Jack."

The bartender would cover the telephone mouthpiece with his hand and whisper to the reporter, "Jack, it's your editor. You here?"

Jack would mouth, "No."

"Sorry, he's not here," the bartender would say.

It was all a code. The reporter would swig down his Manhattan and run back to the office.

Columnist Art Ryon was one of the regulars and used to write restaurant reviews for his column "Ham on Ryon" from the Redwood's front booth. He didn't know much about restaurants so my dad became his leg man and fed him information. Even I made it into his column.

I was maybe 8 or 9 years old and my parents had gone out and left me and my older sister, Sue, at home. I took some steaks out of the freezer and told her I would make us dinner. I didn't know how long the steaks should cook, so I dialed 311, which in those days was the Information line. I asked the operator how long it took to cook a steak, and she laughed. "I don't have that kind of information," she said.

"But this is Information, isn't it?" I persisted.

"Just a minute," she said, "and I'll check with some of the

other operators."

When she returned to the line, I had the answer I needed: "Four minutes on each side."

When I told my father the story, he loved it and passed it on to Art Ryon. The next day, I was the lead story in his column.

The Redwood also attracted politicians, including Governor Pat Brown and Governor Ronald Reagan, as well as high-powered judges, government prosecutors, and private lawyers. It was even rumored that the Redwood served as the inspiration for television lawyer Perry Mason's hangout in the 1957 show based on Erle Stanley Gardner's pulp fiction legal thrillers. Because it was just down the street from the federal court, whenever there was a big trial in downtown LA, local, national and international reporters would gather alongside the attorneys, hoping to get a big scoop to bring back to their newspapers.

Back in the early 1950s, the Shriners, a fraternal organization founded on principles of family and generosity and the founders of the charitable Shriners Hospitals for Children, held a convention in LA. Someone had tied a live camel, which was the organization's mascot, to a lamp post in front of the Redwood. One night, an inebriated columnist went out, untied the camel and rode it into the bar. It took a while but they finally got the camel and its drunken rider out of the restaurant.

In 1963 a young Frank Sinatra, Jr. at the beginning of his career was kidnapped for ransom. He was let go and his kidnappers were caught and tried in 1964. During the trial, all the lawyers and reporters hung out at the Redwood.

Syndicated newspaper gossip columnist Walter Winchell became a regular at the Redwood and always arrived with an entourage, not necessarily because people enjoyed his company but more likely because, as the saying goes, "you should keep your friends close but your enemies closer." And while he considered other reporters "the enemy" he bought them drinks in the hope of obtaining information he could use in his column.

The Redwood was again at the center of the action during the Beverly Hills' Friar's Club trial in the late 1960s. Comedian and actor Milton Berle started the Friars Club as a non-profit, members-only show business club whose members included Bing Crosby, Ronald Reagan, Bob Hope, and Frank Sinatra, to name a few. Later in 1987, Liza Minelli became the first woman to join the Friars. The scandal involved a group of mobsters who were found guilty of cheating celebrities, like Tony Martin and Zeppo Marx, out of hundreds of thousands of dollars in gin rummy by spying on them through peepholes in the ceiling and then somehow transmitting what cards they held to their players, thus making sure they would win.

As much as my dad was a restaurateur, he was also a savvy businessman. Eddie generated a ton of great press for the Redwood House by feeding hungry journalists and giving away countless rounds of drinks. Back in the 1950s while buying pork chops, pork loins, and bacon, he learned the butchers would frequently discard the pork ribs. The suppliers would give him the "spare ribs" for a little charge and sometimes for free when he bought large enough quantities of pork. From this bounty, Smokey Joe's barbecue rib restaurant was born.

My father opened his first Smokey Joe's in 1949 next to Beverly Park, a much- beloved, small amusement park with pony rides on La Cienega and Beverly boulevards where the Beverly Center stands today. At the time, this was a large piece of property, owned by the Hay family, stretching two square city blocks. There were 50 small stores on this massive property but no one had a lease. Rent was paid month-to-month, as there were several producing oil wells just behind the stores so the family didn't want to tie up the land with leases. My father had wanted the corner and spoke to Mr. William Hay. He said he wouldn't give my father a lease but he gave his word that he could be there at least two years. My father took a chance on Mr. Hay's word and built a wooden lean-to structure for the restaurant. My father had 15 years at this corner.

Smokey Joe's across from Beverly Park on the corner of La Cienega and Beverly boulevards, 1963. (Photo from HollywoodHistoricPhotos.com)

The second Smokey Joe's opened in 1952 in North Hollywood's Sherman Oaks neighborhood, about five blocks from the house I grew up in.

The restaurants were so well known there were two chart-topping songs written about them: "Smokey Joe's Café" by lyricist Jerry Leiber and composer Michael Stoller and "Smokey Joe's Barbecue" by Johnny Horton. Leiber and Stoller wrote songs for Elvis Presley and the Coasters and many years later they wrote a Broadway play titled "Smokey Joe's Café."

This is where my 70-year career in the restaurant business began. I was 8 years old. Riverside Drive Elementary was around the corner from Smokey Joe's and every day after school I would walk to the restaurant to work. My first job was to put nickels in the jukebox and play Johnny Horton's "Smokey Joe's Barbecue" over and over again. We had outdoor speakers and I'm sure the entire neighborhood heard the song about 20 times a night. I moved on to folding napkins, peeling carrots, and dreamed of one day achieving my life's greatest ambition: becoming a dishwasher. It seemed like a very adult job to me. My dad was afraid to have me working around all the equipment in the kitchen, so he drew a line on the kitchen wall and said that when I reached the height of the line, I could wash dishes. I checked my height most every day until, one day, I reached the line and became the dishwasher. I was 10 or 11 at the time.

When you work for your father, you take one of two approaches: Either you don't work very hard because you know you won't get fired, or you work twice as hard to prove you didn't get the job because your father owned the place. You can guess which approach I took.

By age 13, I was hosting at Smokey Joe's. I also became my father's bean shill. Always the businessman, my father found a local company to can his Smokey Joe's BBQ (barbequed) beans and he started selling them to grocery stores in the Los Angeles area. It was difficult to get good placement in the neighborhood markets because there weren't any big chains and most of the stores were small grocers and co-ops.

My father and I would go to Gelson's, one of the bigger, upscale markets that carried Smokey Joe's BBQ Beans, and with my father as my lookout, I would rearrange the cans on the shelves by moving some of VanCamp's Baked Beans from the eye-level shelf to a lower level and replace them with Smokey

Joe's BBQ Beans.

Smokey Joe's Menu

When an unsuspecting customer, usually a woman with children, came down the aisle I would loudly beg my father to "please buy me Smokey Joe's Barbequed Beans! They're my favorite food. I'll eat them every night if you buy all of the cans."

He would acquiesce, saying, "Only two, Bob," and put the beans in our cart. Then we'd wheel our cart around the corner and peer back to see if we had convinced the shopper to put our beans into her own cart. It was a ruse that worked a surprising amount of the time.

During the summer when I was 13, I would take the bus downtown to have lunch with my father at the Redwood, which to me, was very exciting. The waitresses who waited on us were nervous to wait on my dad, and I didn't understand their anxiety. After all, it was just my father they were waiting on. Of course, to them, they were waiting on their boss.

One waitress named Josie brought us each a slice of carrot

cake that she had baked at home for dessert. We had never heard of making a cake with carrots. It was just about the best cake either my dad or I had ever tasted. Josie gave us the recipe and I still make the cake to this day. (This recipe is included in the back of this book.)

After lunch we would walk across the street to the California state office building's lawn and toss the football around. This was extra special because nobody was allowed on that lawn, but my father knew all the guards and they let us play. Some of the guards would even play with us.

In the 1950s, Eddie came up with the idea of making frozen sandwiches. Since built-in freezers weren't widespread in grocery stores yet, his frozen Smokey Joe's BBQ Beef sandwiches had to be kept in portable deep freezers and reheated in the oven when ready to be served. While they were successful, the grocery stores would only buy them on consignment, so the more they sold, the deeper my father got in debt, as he had to front the cost. Eventually he sold the sandwich idea to Case Swain, the company that canned the barbeque beans, and received royalties for several years. Case Swain wanted the business because beans were a dry product that could be canned in the winter when they weren't canning fresh vegetables. It kept their business going in the off season. The sandwiches were then sold to a company named Oh Boy which later became Del Monte. A couple of years later, built-in freezers became commonplace in grocery stores and frozen food became all the rage. My father may have been ahead of his time, but not all of his ideas were hits.

Take Bean Cones for example. Gilmore Field, the ballpark for the Hollywood Stars, a minor league baseball team, was located in the same neighborhood as the original Smokey Joe's. My dad started a barbeque cooking show on Sundays between baseball games of a double-header. The show was broadcast live between first and second bases by local television station KTLA. During this time, he came up with the idea of a concession selling sugar-free ice cream style cones filled with his Smokey Joe's barbequed beans at the ballpark. While the cooking show was popular, the Bean Cones, as you can imagine, didn't last a year.

Still, the restaurants did well. In the late 1950s, my father opened a third Smokey Joe's in Santa Monica on Wilshire Boulevard and 25th Street, and a fourth location in the San Fernando Valley. We also had a commissary downtown where we did all of the barbequing. One of my many jobs was delivering food from the commissary to the stores.

When I turned 16, my father bought me a green 1952 Oldsmobile. My job was to drive to the commissary where the beans were cooked and bring them back to the restaurant. One day when I arrived at the commissary, they had run out of the one-gallon jars they used to pack the beans; so, they put them in a four-gallon metal milk can. The milk can was about three feet high and had a very wide opening at the top. They used a coat hanger to secure the lid and turned the can on its side to fit in the trunk of my Oldsmobile and off I went.

When I arrived at the restaurant and opened the trunk, the lid had come off the can and my trunk was awash with about four inches of barbequed beans. I looked around, saw no witnesses, and began to scoop the beans back into the can. At about that time a woman came by. She looked into the trunk and said, "I always wondered how they delivered those barbequed beans." We never did get the smell out of the trunk and finally had to sell the car.

I learned a lot about the restaurant business by watching my father and participating in both the successes and the failures. It's always the failures you learn the most from, although at that time I was too young to appreciate those lessons. What I liked most about the restaurant business was getting to meet the guests and working alongside the adults. I was proud of everything I did. No matter how many hours I worked, I never tired until after the job was done. It was in my genes.

Chapter 2
The Early Years

I was an adventurous kid. The words "slow down" didn't mean much to me.

When I was 6 months old, my 3-year-old sister, Susan, decided to take her "baby" (me) for a walk in my carriage. As she wheeled me down the front steps of our house, she lost control, the carriage turned over, and I fell to the ground. She ran into the house to let mom know "her" baby fell down the steps.

"That's too bad, dear," our mother said, thinking Susan was talking about her doll. Then she heard the howling and found me laying on the sidewalk wearing just a diaper.

When I was about 4 years old, my parents bought me a tricycle, which I rode day after day. When I turned 5, dad converted the trike to a two-wheel bike and took me out to the front yard to show me how to ride it. Not waiting for instruction, I hopped on the bike and took off down the street with my worried father running after me. I rode around the entire block and returned to our front lawn, where, not knowing how to stop, I jumped off the bike and crashed onto the grass.

My gear was always full speed ahead, a trait that probably served me better as a baseball player and entrepreneur than in my early academic years.

I didn't fare so well in the classroom. I attended the Los Angeles Unified School District from kindergarten to first grade. But when we moved to Burbank's school system, because of the way the school year was structured, I ended up repeating first grade. This made me the oldest in my class, which gave me an advantage playing sports in later years. By the time I reached second grade at Riverside Drive Grammar School, my teacher, Miss Stricktland, called my mother in to warn her that "Bobby" was falling way behind.

I would read the first and last letters of a word and my mind would make up the rest, which was usually wrong and out of context with the sentence. I couldn't concentrate on a sentence, paragraph, or even the story. Instead of stopping to go back and figure out what the sentence was about, I just kept going until I was totally lost. I don't even remember really thinking about why I couldn't keep up.

My mother tried everything she knew of to get me help, including taking me to a remedial reading teacher. I was in the sixth grade and only reading at the second-grade level. I had been pushed through the school system. Some of the blame rests with me because although I couldn't always fully comprehend what I read I was smart enough to figure out a way to game the system.

The remedial reading instructor gave me a story to read at the first-grade level. If I answered the follow-up questions correctly, I would move on to the next grade level. I was able to get through the first and second grade level tests but when it came to the third-grade level, I couldn't answer the questions. After noticing the stories were all color-coded, I figured out there was a pattern to the answers: red, blue, green, yellow, and back to red. Once I discovered this, I didn't even have to try to read the stories. I answered the quiz questions using the color code. I was able to answer all the questions up to the sixth-grade level. Based on that, the teacher told my mother I was reading at the sixth-grade level. But really, I was still only at a second-grade level. We tried several other remedial reading instructors to no avail. The harder I tried to make the words make sense, the more scrambled they became.

Years later, as an adult, I learned that I had Dyslexia but, in those days, the experts didn't have any answers. They didn't even understand the problem. During the early 1950s, public school was pretty much "one size fits all." Learning disabilities that are easily identified and treated now weren't defined then. Those who couldn't keep up just got pushed along. That's what happened to me.

My mother even brought me to a psychiatrist, thinking my reading issues were emotional. All I did was lie to him and answer his questions the way I thought he would want to hear them. I always tried to make myself sound good. Nothing helped. I just accepted that I wasn't a very good student and went on with my life.

An example of how dyslexia impacted my daily life is illustrated in what I call the Reddi-Wip incident. When I was about 7 years old, I wanted to put whipped cream on my strawberry shortcake. I read the directions on the can: "Do not puncture." All I saw was "puncture" so I took an ice pick and jammed it into the aerosol can. The container exploded and whipped cream spewed all over the walls, the ceiling, and everywhere else. I swiped the whipped cream off the wall with my finger and ate it. Then I called my mother to tell her what I had done.

I was 8 years old when my parents bought their first home in 1951 in a new subdivision in Sherman Oaks, the iconic Birdhouse Ranch Homes built by developer William Mellenthin, who constructed hundreds of post-war homes in the east San Fernando Valley. Sixteen thousand dollars bought a three-bedroom, two-bath house with a birdhouse on the garage roof.

Most of the houses in our neighborhood had kids the same ages as my sister and me. We played driveway basketball or street football. Cars would have to wait until the play was over before we'd step aside and let them through. But none of the drivers seemed to care about waiting; they just watched the game.

Spring and summer we'd play baseball on a vacant lot. Jack Handley, a friend who lived directly behind me, and I were the two best players in the neighborhood. Jack's father was a professional baseball player and Jack was a good athlete as well. We would alternate choosing players for the two teams. Some of those players were orphans from the nearby McKinley Home for Boys. I came to know a few of them quite well and heard stories of what it was like living in an orphanage. There was no adult supervision at our games, just a bunch of kids working it out on the field of play. I guess that's where my love of baseball began.

Our games would last until five o'clock, when we all had to go home for dinner. None of our mothers worked at outside jobs, so they cooked dinner every night. As kids, we never had any say in what we had for dinner; we just ate everything mom made. Dad may have been in the restaurant business but mom was the real cook in the family, and, for the time, something of a health fanatic; she never took any medication. In the early 1950s my mother was concerned about bread containing preservatives, so she didn't buy it. Also, whenever we ate anything with fat in it, we had to drink a hot drink. She thought that would help "melt" the fat and not clog our veins.

We ate red meat and creamy casseroles every meal and also had fresh vegetables. There were several standard menu items my mother would make for dinner: Tuna Casserole with crushed up potato chips on top, Meatloaf, and an item she called Mexican Scrabble consisting of hamburger and tomato sauce topped with crispy tortillas.

Mom, Sue, and I would sit down to dinner as a family and talk about our day: school, the afternoon ball game, and current events. My father rarely had dinner with us; he worked at the restaurant every night. My mother was very interested in Democratic politics, and I grew up interested in politics as well.

In 1952, Adlai Stevenson was the Democratic candidate running against Republican Dwight D. Eisenhower. I can remember going to the Democrat headquarters and getting a free campaign button and bumper sticker which I put on my bike. I was amazed you could just go to the Democratic headquarters and get free stickers and buttons! This was before television. Mom would listen to Walter Winchell on the radio and I listened with her. To this day, I have a love for Democratic politics.

While my father's business practices sometimes bordered on "creative," my mother's ingrained ethics balanced the scales. Around this time my mother gave me a 50-cent piece and sent me to the five-and-ten-cent store to buy nail polish for her. Before I left, she warned, "Now don't drop it," knowing that I tended to toss anything I was carrying into the air and catch it like a pop-fly at the bottom of the ninth inning with bases loaded.

Sure enough, on the way home I threw that little bottle into the air. Up, up it went, and then down and...shattered on the sidewalk. I missed the catch. Not wanting to face my mother, I returned to the store, took another bottle off the shelf, put it in my pocket, and left without paying for it.

That night, I woke up at 3 a.m., crying uncontrollably. When my mother came to my room to see what was wrong, I confessed my guilt. Her son was a thief! She said we would talk in the morning, then put me back to bed. I never went back to sleep. Instead, I worried about the coming morning's inevitable *talk*.

As a little boy, I never wanted to get into trouble, and I still don't today.

The next morning, Mother laid out her plan: we would go to the store and I would tell the manager what I had done. I would apologize and pay for the stolen bottle with money that she would lend me. I, of course, would have to repay the loan. I did this by forfeiting my 25-cent allowance for the next two weeks. I learned my lesson and never did anything like that again. My mother was the most ethical person I have ever known. As an adult, I always faced critical decisions with my mother's ethics in mind.

Now, my mother was very frugal. She would take the money for each month and divide it into separate envelopes to pay the bills: mortgage, groceries, haircuts, lunch, clothing for me and my sister, etc. While my mother was counting pennies my father was spending it on whatever he wanted, whenever he wanted. He had a closet full of silk suits. This had to be a real problem for my mother. She realized she was unhappy and started seeing a psychiatrist. In 1952, this was very unusual and brave of her. She had reached her breaking point.

One night when I was about 10 years old, I woke up around 1 a.m. to hear my mother and father arguing. It's really the only time I remember ever hearing them argue. My dad worked long hours. He would leave the house at 9 a.m. and not come home until after midnight. He did this six days a week. On Sundays he would sleep most of the day. It wasn't until years later that I realized he was also unhappy in the marriage and would rather stay at the Redwood House and work than come home.

The argument was over a letter my mother had written to my father—a letter expressing her frustration with their marriage—a letter that was never meant to be sent. When my father arrived home from the restaurant, he found the letter and read it.

In January 1953, my mother sat Sue and me down and informed us that she and our father were getting a divorce.

"We're going to be a family of three. We're going to travel and go to Hawaii," she told us. I remember those words as if it were yesterday. At the time, going to Hawaii was as big of a deal as any 10-year-old kid could dream of. It would be like going to the moon today. (We never made it to Hawaii.) Then she said, "If you hear anyone trying to break into the house tonight, don't get scared. It's only your father. I had the locks changed on the doors."

I stayed awake all night, waiting to hear my dad come home. When he came back to the house late that night, all his silk suits were on the lawn. I watched from the front window as my father gathered up his suits and put them into the car. He never did try to come into the house.

Those suits meant a lot to my father. He grew up in Boyle Heights, a very poor part of town. To him, those suits were a symbol of success; he had made it out of Boyle Heights to the mainstream of Los Angeles.

That night he stayed at a motel and the next day he rented an apartment at the Holiday Manor, about a mile from our house. I guess he realized how serious my mother was about getting a divorce.

I think this was the first time I ever heard the word "divorce." It scared me. I thought for sure I would be going to live at the McKinley Home for Boys. The next morning, when some of the kids came by my house to walk to school together, I told them I wasn't going to school that day because I was becoming an orphan. I was so upset that my mother let me stay home from school.

The divorce woke my father up to the fact that if he didn't try harder, he was going to lose his kids. He took an apartment near our house and made a real effort. Although I never doubted my father's love for me, he just wasn't around very much because he worked all the time. I stayed with him over the weekends.

It was around that time when mother sent me to camp for two weeks: the Lazy J in Canoga Park. Today, Canoga Park is a large residential part of the West San Fernando Valley but in 1953 it was nothing but farms and agriculture. From the day I got to camp I was homesick. I cried all day long.

The camp was owned by Mr. and Mrs. Johnson and we called them Mr. and Mrs. J. The second day of crying, Mrs. J gave me the job of sweeping her very large brick patio. This kept me busy and stopped me from crying. The camp had farm animals and each camper chose one of the animals to take care of. Since I cried the first two days, I didn't get a chance to choose my animal and had to take what was leftover, which happened to be a pig. When I smelled the pig pen, I knew why nobody had picked the pig! I hated that job and started crying again.

Fortunately, the fourth day they took all the campers to a rodeo, which was a lot of fun. At the end of the rodeo, they brought all the Lazy J kids to the arena for a foot race. I was in the younger group, ages 9 and 10, and I won the race. My counselor then bet the counselor of the 11- and 12-year-old kids that I could beat his fastest runner in a race. I won that race too, which made me popular with the other campers and I forgot how homesick I was. By the end of the second week, I was voted "Best Camper" and awarded a T-shirt imprinted with those words.

Both of my parents started dating almost immediately. In that era, having parents dating was unusual, but I just accepted it as normal. Dad wanted me and Sue to meet his girlfriend, Rosemary. We met for dinner at the Sportsmen's Lodge in Studio City. The Lodge was next to a pond stocked with trout and you could rent a fishing pole, catch a fish, and the chef would cook it for you. I dressed up in black slacks and a white dinner jacket and I remember pulling the chair out to seat Rosemary. Other than this introduction, my father didn't include us in his relationship like people do now. Not too much later after that dinner, he called from Mexico to say that he and Rosemary had gotten married. Rather than feeling hurt, I just accepted it. My sister didn't take it that well. She was three years older than me and resented dad's new wife. She didn't have much of a relationship with our father after that.

My mother went out with several men but nobody serious. One day, Rosa Schlobohm, who played cards with my mother, told her about a neighbor: a widower with two daughters, Jody, 12, and Louise, 9. His name was Deane Ames and Rosa wanted my mother to meet him. He had been single for two years and had dated several women, though no one he became interested in. When mom and Deane met, it was love at first sight. To finalize a divorce in California in 1953, you had to wait a year. Dad and Rosemary couldn't wait and went to Mexico to get married. Mom, however, had to do it the legal way. She moved to Las Vegas for six weeks to establish residency, and the day her Nevada divorce was final, she married Deane.

Overnight, I went from having one sister to three. Mom and Deane remodeled our house, adding a master bedroom and a large family room. Mom made sure that our house was open to all our friends, and the family room was like a clubhouse for all the kids in the neighborhood to gather.

There was a big adjustment putting two families with four children, aged 9 to 14, together. Jody was in ninth grade at Van Nuys Junior High School, and I was starting seventh grade. We rode the bus together to school, and she showed me the ropes.

Jody and Louise were excellent students, I was only interested in athletics, and Sue was boy crazy. Somehow, thanks to Mom and Deane, we all accepted the relationship. In those days, a blended family like ours was unusual, especially one that got along as well as the four of us did. That's just the way it was. After almost 70 years, we still talk on the phone regularly and see each other when we can.

As well as I got along with my new sisters, Deane and I had a different relationship. To his credit, Deane was good at accepting his role of stepfather. He was a nice man, but I really had nothing in common with him. He'd take me fishing, something I didn't really care for, but I went along because that's what was expected of me. One time he took me to the Los Angeles Civic Light Opera, again, something he wanted to do that I didn't particularly care for. After two years of this, I went to my mother. "I've done everything Deane likes to do but he doesn't do anything I like to do."

"Like what?" my mother asked.

"Throwing a baseball around or going to a baseball game," I answered.

It wasn't a half hour later when Deane said, "Let's go in the backyard and throw a baseball around." I threw the ball hard and broke his finger. That was the end of "let's do what Bob likes to do." Despite that incident, we still loved and respected one another. I think he just realized we were very different and that was okay. He also knew I had a father who I was very close to and he never tried to interfere with that relationship. I could see my dad anytime I wanted and vice versa. There were no forced visitation rules.

My mother's friend, Mildred Schwartz, and her husband

Sherwood often visited us at the house and would marvel at how well the four of us kids got along. Sherwood kept asking us questions about what it was like to bring two families together as one. Fifteen years later, in 1969, "The Brady Bunch" began its five-season run on ABC-TV, with Sherwood Schwartz as the producer. Our family, he told our parents, was the inspiration for the show.

Through all these changes, baseball was always there for me. When I turned 9, I was able to sign up for Little League. By that time, I was a very good player for my age as I had been playing with boys who were a year or two older. My father took me to United Sporting Goods in downtown Los Angeles to buy my first adult mitt. He refused the salesman's offer of a kid's mitt, saying, "My boy is much more advanced and needs a mitt an adult would use." The salesman brought out the mitt, and as my father and I played catch in the store, the salesman realized what my dad knew all along; I could handle the adult mitt. My confidence ran high that day; I felt my father's pride with every soft thud of the ball that landed squarely in the pocket of the glove. I made the team and got my first baseball uniform, with number 2 on the back – definitely the highlight of my young life.

Despite my struggles with school and my parents' divorce, my home life was good and I never felt different from the other kids.

Chapter 3
Sports...and Girls...and Sports

I was 13 years old when I entered seventh grade at Van Nuys Junior High School. In the Jewish faith, 13 is considered the age where boys become men and accept their religious obligations through a Bar Mitzvah ceremony. Many of my friends were learning Hebrew in preparation for the ceremony and I tried to study Hebrew but had to drop out; I had enough trouble learning English. Accordingly, I was unable to be Bar Mitzvahed. This was not a big problem as I didn't grow up with many Jewish families. As a matter of fact, I was not invited to many Bar Mitzvah's growing up. Sports continued to be my focus and salvation. That, and a new distraction – girls!

In school, I took Choir class and deliberately altered my voice to sound higher so I could be in the Soprano section – because that's where the girls were! My first junior high girlfriend was Joanie. We played Spin-the-Bottle at parties and I was always glad when the bottle pointed to Joanie.

One day when school let out and everyone streamed out the doors to catch the bus, I happened to be walking out the doors with Leslie, the most popular girl in school. I was in the eighth grade, and she was in ninth. We started talking and before I knew it, we passed the waiting buses and continued walking away from the school. I didn't mind missing the bus that day even though I knew there was no chance she would date me; she was going steady with a high school boy who drove a red Corvette convertible, but Leslie was so friendly that we just kept on walking and talking for about an hour until we reached her street. At that point, I didn't want her to know how far out of the way I had walked, so I said goodbye and walked back to my house...3 miles! The detour was well worth it.

Van Nuys Junior High School had a special area, the Ninth Grade Lawn, where only ninth graders could congregate. I would stand on the edge of the grass and watch Leslie talking with all her friends. They seemed to be having such a great time, but I could only watch from the sidelines. On my first day as a ninth grader, I couldn't wait to go on the Lawn with my friends. By then Leslie had moved on to high school. We went to different high schools and I didn't see her again until many years later.

I played baseball in the Babe Ruth League, which was for 13- to 15-year-olds. My first year we played a team whose star pitcher was a kid named Don Calabria. I only knew him by reputation: he was one of the best pitchers in the entire league. Every time I came up to bat, it seemed like he was throwing the ball at me. One pitch hit me in the shoulder. After the game was over, I confronted him and asked if he was intentionally trying to hit me. He said yes, because I was dating his ex-girlfriend, Sherry.

Sherry was my first love. We dated in the last year of junior high but when we went to high school, I wanted to date other girls and we broke up. After the breakup, Don and I became best friends, and still are to this day.

I was in the ninth grade when my youngest sister, Louise, entered seventh grade and I was able to show her around the way our older sister Jody did for me. Louise and Jody were great students, far better than me. I used to tease Louise and inevitably she'd end up in tears. Despite the teasing, Louise was proud that her big brother was a well-known school athlete.

That last year of junior high I played in the faculty- student All-Star football game. A 300-pound teacher ran into me and fractured a bone in my neck. The injury kept me out of contact sports for about six months which included the rest of the year and into the fall of high school.

Even as I excelled in sports, academics continued to be a challenge. By the time I entered the tenth grade at Van Nuys High School in 1959, my friends were taking foreign languages, higher math, and all the classes necessary for college. I tried taking those classes, too, but only fell further behind. My high school counselor, coaches, and parents got together to discuss what they should do with my schoolwork. After years of trying to get help for my learning problems, my mother believed I should give up on college preparatory classes and take more practical courses that would help me as an adult and keep my grades up so I could remain eligible to play football.

I was good at basic math, interested in Social Studies, and struggled through English. I took Bookkeeping, Typing, and Print Shop. I learned a lot about bookkeeping and how to read a financial report, as well as a balance sheet, which served me well when I got into business and had my own restaurants. In later years I realize I had the last laugh because what's more important today; algebra or typing?

There was one aspect of school I really enjoyed; agriculture class. I liked planting vegetables and watching them grow. I checked my vegetables every day and looked forward to harvesting and eating the tomatoes. The class would also deliver the extra produce to a poor area in Van Nuys and it made me feel good we were able to provide good food to people who couldn't afford to buy fresh vegetables.

Since I was sidelined from playing sports that first semester, I had time to work at Smokey Joe's every day after school. I was now the prep cook. I cut vegetables and made all the side dishes. At night I was the host. I learned how to seat people at different servers' stations so they would be able to concentrate on each party seated in their section. That was a win because the guests received better service and were apt to leave larger tips. The restaurant had 20 tables and six booths. Everyone wanted to sit in a booth. Later, when I opened my own restaurants, I knew how important it was to have more booths than tables with chairs.

I worked until 8 p.m. most days and then got up at 7 a.m. for school each morning. Back then, white peggers (jeans that tapered at the ankle), as they were called then, were popular with kids my age and, of course, I wanted a pair. My mother told me the only way I could get a pair of white pants was if I washed and ironed them myself. So, along with getting up early just to get ready for school, I also had to iron the white pants I had washed the night before.

My sister Jody, now a senior, along with several of my neighborhood friends who were a year ahead of me, showed me how to get around in high school, which made the transition from junior high a lot easier.

One thing the boys showed me was how to cut class without getting caught. We would check into a class and when the teacher wasn't looking, walk out the back door. I also made sure my mother never signed anything from school. Whenever a parent had to sign anything, I would sign her name. Later, when I missed a whole day of school, I could write my own excuse, sign my mother's name, and no one was the wiser. My mother never found out. I was a willing participant; anything to get out of class. Looking back, I'm not proud of those days but this is what I did.

It was around this same time I acquired the nickname of Angle. I could always come up with an "angle" or excuse when one of us was about to get into trouble. If we were going to get home after curfew, I'd come up with an excuse on why we were late: flat tire, car wouldn't start, one of our friends was sick. If one of my friends didn't get their homework done, they would call me for an excuse like "the exterminator tented our house and I couldn't get in to get my homework." I had the ability to "think on my feet" and while that had dubious applications during my school years, it served me well in business later on.

Because of the injury I sustained in the faculty All-Star game in junior high I wasn't able to play football, which was what I really wanted to do. Instead, I went out for Basketball which was considered a minor sport in the late 1950s. Basketball practice was the last period of the day. The coach never gave me a chance to make the team so I stopped going. He never even missed me. When it came time to get a grade in the Basketball class, I told the coach I was at practice every day. The basketball team won the league championship that year and so the coach gave everyone an A — including me. I still can't believe I got away with that.

Baseball season arrived in the second semester. I was pretty well healed from my injury by then and was able to play. All of my older friends were on the team. When the coach told me that I not only had made the team but would be the starting first baseman, I was so excited the first thing I did was find a pay phone to call my father. My father was excited and said, "I knew you would make the team!"

My older friends explained that on game days we never went to school after lunch. That meant we had to cut the last two classes of the day. Again, they showed me how to do it and not get caught.

During the early 1950s, Los Angeles didn't have a major league baseball team, but we did have two Pacific Coast League AAA teams: the Hollywood Stars and the Los Angeles Angels. These teams were often called the third major league because the level of baseball was so good.

The Stars, a Pittsburgh Pirates farm team, were owned by Bob Hope, Bing Crosby, and several other big entertainers. Our next-door neighbor, Gene Handley, played second base for the Stars. Mr. Handley would sometimes ask me to fill in as bat boy which involved carrying baseball bats out to the players. Being in the dugout with these professional players was exciting and fueled my dream to one day take my place on the field with them.

My favorite major league team as a kid was the Brooklyn Dodgers. I'm not sure why, though looking back I believe it was because they had signed Jackie Robinson, the first Black major leaguer, who became one of my idols. The Dodgers moved to LA in 1958. Before Dodger Stadium was built in Chavez Ravine, the team played in the Los Angeles Coliseum, which was built for football, not baseball. This was not ideal, but now we had real major league baseball!

On May 7, 1959, I was 15 years old when the Dodgers played an exhibition game to honor their catcher, Roy Campanella, who had been in a car accident and was paralyzed from the waist down. There were over 93,000 fans at the coliseum to honor Roy and it was the largest crowd to ever see a Major League baseball game. During the seventh-inning stretch, they turned off the lights, and all those people stood up and held a lighter or lit match. You could feel the outpouring of love for this man. To this day, I can close my eyes and remember how it felt to be part of that moment, part of something bigger than myself.

Saturday nights were for dating and I don't think I ever failed to have a date. Other times, me and the guys I played baseball with—Don, Jack, John, Mike, and George—would drive down Van Nuys Boulevard in my 1952 Oldsmobile to Bob's Big Boy restaurant, the local high school hang out.

We'd cruise through the parking lot at about five miles an hour to see who was there, then find a place to park, order food and talk to the other carloads of kids. The waitresses were called "car hops" and wore roller skates, just like at Arnolds, the fictional restaurant in "Happy Days." They'd roll around the cars, take orders and deliver food on plastic trays that hooked on the side of a partially rolled-down car window.

Sometimes you'd be ready to leave and your car wouldn't start, either because it was an old clunker or you left the radio on and drained the battery. To a teenage boy, this was a fate worse than death! Everyone would stare as you pushed your car out of the parking lot. This happened to me more than once.

Bob's Big Boy had several restaurants located near high schools; it was a successful formula. One thing I learned at Bob's, which stuck with me, was the great feeling when the server or manager called me by name. It made me feel very special. Another thing that impressed me was how clean Bob's kept the restrooms. Later, when I had my own restaurants, I taught everyone how important it was to recognize people by name and keep the bathrooms clean.

After Van Nuys High's baseball season was over, we played on the All-Star team in the Colt League, which was for 16- and 17-year-olds. Once again, along with my older friends, we were the stars of the league. We were in the Western Colt League All-Star tournament and needed to win five games in a row to go to the Colt League World Series in San Diego. We won the first four games and then it was down to the final game. That game went into the last inning. Don was pitching. The score was tied 0-0. In the bottom of the ninth inning, I took four balls and walked to first base, stole second and third bases, and made it to home plate, scoring the winning run on a sacrifice fly. We won the game 1-0. We were headed for San Diego!

For all of us, this was our first time away from home — and did it show! We stayed in the barracks at the Marine Corps Miramar Air Station. While the other teams were in bed at 10 p.m., we stayed up and played cards all night. The next day when it came time to play, we were dead tired. Our opponents, meanwhile, were rested and ready to go. We lost. Badly. What I learned from that experience is that *if you don't prepare, you don't achieve.* That's a lesson that stayed with me the rest of my life.

My career at Van Nuys High School was interrupted in the eleventh grade with a transfer to U.S. Grant High School, a new school that had just opened. While half of my junior class was transferred, the seniors were allowed to stay on at Van Nuys so they could graduate from the school they had attended the past two years. I was now separated from my older friends and teammates I had grown up with. This made it hard for us to compete in sports because we lost those older, more experienced members of our team. But like most changes in life, transferring to U.S. Grant was a blessing in disguise.

I met a girl named Andy who had transferred to Grant from a neighboring school. Andy and I started dating and went steady for the entire eleventh grade year. Andy was very pretty and came from North Hollywood High School where her brother was the student body president. I tried out for the football team and became one of its best players. Andy went from being the sister of the school president to the girlfriend of the school's star football player – yes, me! After the student-faculty football incident in junior high, my mother felt football was too dangerous and didn't want me to play in high school. I wouldn't take "no" for an answer and told her the first time I got hurt I'd quit.

And so it happened: the first game of the season, second quarter, I got kicked in the head. The rest of the game was a blur. By the end of the game, I was feeling OK, and the team doctor told me to come into his office the next morning at 8 a.m. Of course, I didn't tell my mother about the injury, but she found out anyway. While I was at the doctor's office, she received eight phone calls asking how I was feeling. When I got back from the doctor, she tried to get me to quit, but that wasn't going to happen and I stayed on the team. Even though we didn't win a lot of games that first year, I had achieved the status of being a football star and along with that came the admiration from fellow students. As a kid who lacked academic success, this was a great way to be accepted by the other kids in my class.

Despite my struggles in school and a reputation as an outstanding athlete, I realized sports shouldn't be the only measure of success, a lesson I learned from the football team manager.

Henry Weinstein was the guy who ran the water out to the team during timeouts. He was also the kid Coach Johnny always made fun of because Henry was small and not a very good athlete. All Henry wanted was to be a part of the team. The coach would say "Here comes Henry. He is going to trip over the chalk line." I remember thinking how messed up the system was. After all, Henry was the smartest student in the school; he should have been the star of the stars in high school, not ridiculed.

Through diet and hard work, Henry transformed himself and went on to make the junior varsity cross-country team and the varsity team in his senior year, which was a year after I graduated. Henry attended U.C. Berkley law school and worked over 30 years at the *Los Angeles Times* covering law, labor, and politics. Currently, he's a professor at the University of California-Irvine where he teaches media law.

Throughout the years, I never forgot about Henry and the

way Coach had treated him. About 40 years later I was having dinner with my good friend Marylouise Oates, who had also been a writer for the Times. I asked Marylouise, or "Oatsie" as she is known to her friends, if she knew Henry Weinstein. She told me they talked on the phone all the time. I asked her to do me a favor and invite him over for dinner but not tell him I was going to be there. Oatsie set it up and when I walked into her home, Henry was there, sitting on the couch. He immediately recognized me and we hugged each other. We both had tears in our eyes. He was as excited to see me as I was to see him. I told him I knew he was the smartest student in the school and that we, meaning the football players, should have been shining his shoes. Henry was just happy to see me and let me know he understood. It was a great night.

By the end of football season, Coach Johnny, who also coached track, had noticed that I was the fastest runner on the team. He told me, "I guess we know who is going to be the sprinter on the track team."

"Not me, Coach," I said. "I play baseball."

He thought for a second then said, "The baseball games are on Tuesdays and Thursdays. Track meets are on Fridays. What if I talk to the baseball coach and have him let you out of practice on Fridays to run in the track meets?"

That was fine with me, and that's just what we did. I won both the 100- and 220-yard dash in each of our first nine track meets. Our tenth and last meet was against Van Nuys, my old school, where all my old friends were seniors. Their sprinter was considered the best sprinter in the San Fernando Valley. He had won all his races and had been the champion sprinter the previous year.

Even though my father worked very hard, he always found time to leave work at the Redwood and attend my football and baseball games. Now, thanks to the football coach, he had to attend all the track meets as well. My father was my biggest fan.

Just before the 100-yard dash my dad started talking with the man standing next to him, who mentioned that his son but the fastest runner in the race. My dad never said a word. After the race, which I won, my father turned to the man and smiled broadly. "That was my son who won the race." I went on to also win the 220-yard race. Winning the San Fernando championship allowed me to run in the Los Angeles City High School finals, where I finished third in both races.

With varsity letters in football, baseball, and track, I became known as the star athlete of the school. In my senior year the sportswriters in the San Fernando Valley voted me in as the running back on the All-League team. I also made the All-League team as first baseman on the varsity baseball team and was the sprint champion of the San Fernando Valley. My father attended every one of my athletic events so he also became well-known on campus. He had never graduated from high school and was thrilled by my success as well as being recognized as my dad. I can never remember a time when my dad wasn't proud of me.

***

Looking back, I realized that even with all the learning problems, I had a good self-image. My parents were supportive and athletics made me very popular in both junior and senior high school. Nobody even knew or thought about my grades or the fact that I was never in their algebra, geometry, or Spanish classes.

I was ashamed of my learning problems and became adept at hiding them from my friends and the rest of my family. Years later, when I was able to talk about my learning problems, I asked a few people I went to school with if they knew what a poor student I was. The answer was always the same: "No, we didn't know. We just liked you for who you were."

When my sisters Jody and Louise read a draft of this chapter, they were both surprised; neither one of them knew of my problems. It was never discussed at home or with my friends. I'm not saying that the way I moved through the grades without obtaining a higher level of comprehension and learning was right, it's just the way it was. I guess I repressed it so much I can't even remember how I felt. I'm not saying this is a good thing, but somehow it seemed to work for me. Some people might say that at some time I would end up on a psychiatrist's couch discussing how I had repressed these feelings, but I never did. Here I am, 80 years old, feeling happy and content with my life and relationships with my children, wife, and friends.

***

During my senior year spring break, my father and Rosemary took our family to Palm Springs. It was there I met Beth Brody, who would become my steady girlfriend through the rest of high school. Beth was two years behind me and attending Van Nuys High School. I found out later that before we met, she had cut a picture of me out of the newspaper and hung it on her bulletin board. So, when we were introduced to each other she already knew who I was.

The summer after I graduated from high school, my dad hired a private batting instructor hoping to improve my batting by teaching me how to attack the ball and hit it hard. Ray Poitevint had been a professional baseball player. I worked with Ray the entire summer of 1961 and finally learned to hit the baseball with power. Unfortunately, one time Ray was pitching to me, I hit a line drive so hard it hit him in the middle of his forehead. I rushed him to the emergency hospital where he was diagnosed with a serious concussion. My batting lessons ended there and Ray went on to become a famous scout for the Baltimore Orioles baseball team.

That same summer, I qualified as a sprinter on the United States Maccabiah team. The Maccabiah games were like the Olympic games for Jewish athletes. Their charter was to promote fitness and athleticism for Jewish youth and to strengthen Jewish bonds and create heightened awareness of Israel. There were 26 countries in the competition, which took place in Tel Aviv, Israel every four years.

My parents brought me up in the Jewish faith and culture and even though I didn't attend Temple regularly, I had a strong emotional attachment to the culture. I had just turned 18 and had never been overseas on my own. I didn't know anybody on the team. We flew to New York and on to Tel Aviv, where we stayed in the Olympic Village in Ramat Gan Tel Aviv. The South African team also stayed on our floor. I never realized that South Africa had a large Jewish community. We spent the 10 days there with their team.

One of the things we loved to do was to go the entrance of the Olympic Village where we were staying and sign autographs for the Israeli kids who would wait for us.

At about this time, Adidas was building its athletic shoe brand by giving away pairs of red, white, and blue Track shoes to American athletes competing in international events; our whole team proudly wore Adidas athletic shoes.

For most of the two weeks I was quite homesick. I missed Beth and my family. Beth and my mother and dad wrote to me every day. But when the sporting events started, my mind focused on the competition.

I finished second in the 100-meter dash. When it came time for the 200-meter race I had a real problem – all the starting commands were in Hebrew and I didn't understand what the starter was saying. I just figured the first thing he said was, "Runners get on your marks" and everyone would take their place at the starting blocks. The second command would be "Get set" and we'd crouch down, place our hands on the starting line and position our feet against the starting blocks. However, this time there was no second command. The starter told us to start over. I didn't understand so I crouched down to get set. I looked around and all the other runners were standing up. That's when I realized he had called us off our marks.

The same thing happened the second time and I stood up again. The third time the starter was getting impatient and said, in Hebrew, "get set" and then fired the gun to go. But after the previous false starts, I thought he had called us off our marks for a third time so when the gun went off, I was standing straight up and the other runners were already running. I took off and caught up to everyone except the runner from Canada, who won the race. I finished second again and came home with two silver medals. On the way home, the plane stopped at the Paris Airport and I bought Beth a bottle of Chanel No. 5 perfume; it was the only brand name I recognized.

For the rest of that summer, I worked out with Ray and played baseball for a Dodger rookie team. The Dodgers were looking to possibly sign me to a minor league contract. After playing in about six games, I realized that as good I had been in high school, these guys were much better ball players than I would ever be. Ray had told me, "If they don't think you're good enough to offer you a bonus to sign, they don't think you'll make it to the majors." This realization ended my dream of playing in the big leagues.

Chapter 4
The Redwood

I had barely graduated from high school and, with the glory days of my sporting years behind me, it was time to get serious about my career. I started working full-time at my father's restaurant, the Redwood House, in downtown Los Angeles.

Historical photo found in Eddie Spivak's papers of the Redwood location, 1950s, at the corner of First Street and Broadway in downtown LA. The Redwood House is sandwiched between the two buildings on the right. The LA Times building is visible from the left.

At the time, I was still living at home with my mother and now that I was drawing a paycheck, she thought I should be responsible and pay rent. Unfortunately, responsibility was a lesson I wasn't ready to learn. I moved out of the house and went to live with my father and Rosemary, where I didn't have to pay rent. I'm sure this hurt my mother, but she never mentioned it. And if this added to her grievances about my father, I never knew about that either. I think she decided my relationship with my father was more important. (Looking back, I wish we had discussed her feelings, but we never did.)

I worked as bartender, host, and manager, learning all aspects of the restaurant business, including how to manage important guests like the columnists, politicians, lawyers and judges who regularly dined with us, a skill that would be essential two decades later in my own business.

The restaurant had a fancy bar and dining room called the Red Garter Room, which my father was in charge of. This room had red-flocked wallpaper, red carpet, black leather booths, and low lighting that created an alluring ambiance; everyone wanted to sit in the Red Garter Room. There was seating for about 50 people at the tables and another 20 at the bar.

Eddie Spivak with bar manager, Bill Eaton, at the Redwood's Red Garter Room in 1970. The LA Times took over the building for offices, and the restaurant moved to a new location. This photo was taken on the day of demolition in the original location. The LA Times article described the Redwood as "a retreat for the Civic Centers' famous and infamous for nearly three decades.

The Redwood also had a coffee shop and another 100-person dining room in the rear of the restaurant. This was the room I was in charge of. Bailiffs from the nearby Los Angeles County Courthouse would regularly bring jurors over for lunch.

We were able to seat all 12 jurors and two bailiffs at a long table in a corner of the dining room for privacy. The Redwood was a popular lunch spot for employees from the Los Angeles City Hall, the California State Building, the Los Angeles County Hall of Records, the courthouses, and reporters from the *Los Angeles Times*. Those who were lucky enough would be directed to the Red Garter Room by my father. The others would sit in my dining room. From my experience hosting at Smokey Joe's, I knew how to balance the room so each server had the same number of guests and manage the timing so none of the servers had more than one table at a time. That way, the servers could give their best service without being overloaded.

One day in 1966, my dad left me in charge of seating for the Red Garter Room. A man came to the door at 11 a.m. and asked for my father. I explained that Eddie wasn't there, but I was his son. Could I help him? He introduced himself as Harry Cohen, the brother of Mickey Cohen. Now, at that time, Mickey Cohen was the head of the Mafia on the West Coast. When Bugsy Siegel wanted to develop Las Vegas in the 1940s, he had to get permission from Mickey Cohen.

Harry told me his brother was in prison at Alcatraz and had been brought to Los Angeles for trial. Mickey had brought a lawsuit against the federal government for not protecting him in prison from a brutal beating that had paralyzed him from the waist down. Because he was in custody but technically not in prison while in Los Angeles, Mickey didn't have to eat prison food. Harry told me he wanted three orders each of: the biggest New York steaks, medium rare; baked potatoes; mashed potatoes; creamed spinach; steamed broccoli; chocolate cake; and apple pie; plus, three of anything else I wanted to add. He would be back in an hour to pick the food up. He added, "Don't worry about the price. We just want the best there is."

I went to the kitchen and told the chef what I needed, and to take special care in cutting the New York steak from the middle of the sirloin, not from the end, and to cook them a perfect medium rare. Then I asked the Pantry Chef to prepare three servings each of the following: baked potatoes with sour cream and chives, broccoli with cheese sauce, French fried potatoes, mashed potatoes, and creamed spinach. I then asked Alice, the waitress behind the counter, to get me three pieces of chocolate cake, three pieces of apple pie, plus three orders of our special rice pudding, and have it all wrapped up and ready to go in one hour.

At exactly noon, Harry came back to pick up the food. The bill came to $85; a huge sum at the time. He gave me a one-hundred-dollar bill, told me to keep the change, and off he went. He wasn't gone five minutes when the chef came out of the kitchen and said, "Bob, when do you want these steaks?"

"Oh shit!" I exclaimed. I had given Harry Cohen everything but the steaks. "I'll take them now!" The chef gave me the steaks, already plated, on a large metal tray.

I ran outside, hailed a cab, and told the cab driver to take me to the federal courthouse and make it fast. When I arrived, I ran up the stairs with the tray and the three New York steaks.

When I got to the bailiff, I told him my story. After he stopped laughing, he checked the tray and said, "Come with me." He took me to the fifth floor and I followed him down a hallway lined with rows and rows of cells. It looked just like a scene in a Hollywood movie. We stopped at a cell, the bailiff took out a ring of keys, unlocked the door, pushed me in, and slammed the door shut. All I heard was a "clink clink" and there I was, in a prison cell with Mickey Cohen. And, I had arrived ahead of his brother!

Mickey Cohen (in a wheelchair) outside the federal courthouse in downtown Los Angeles January 31, 1966. (Photo from AlcatrazHistory.com)

Mickey was in a wheelchair in the far corner of the cell and gave me a "what are you doing here, kid?" look.

I told him the story and said, "Mr. Cohen, when the chef said 'when do you want these steaks' my whole life flashed before me, and I knew I had to deliver them to you."

Mickey chuckled. Just about that time, his brother and his lawyer came into the cell. They were certainly surprised to see me.

When I got back to the restaurant all hell had broken loose because with me gone, there wasn't anyone to direct the people back to my dining room and they all sat in the Red Garter Room. I didn't have any open tables for the regulars. Everyone was mad at me, but I had lived to seat the room another day.

After I had been seating people for a year or so, my father wanted me to learn how to tend bar. This was tricky, given all the hard-drinking reporters from the *Los Angeles Times* who used the bar as a second office.

One time we had a fire in the kitchen and I needed to get the bar customers outside for safety.

"Fire in the kitchen!" I yelled. "Everyone out of the bar!" Nobody moved.

Then I said, "Leave the bar until we find out if the fire is serious. When you come back, I'll buy everyone a drink."

That did it. Everyone jumped up and ran outside.

My dad employed a dishwasher by the name of Tomas. Every year or so, Tomas would leave his job without telling anyone and go back to Mexico to visit his family. When he returned, he never said a word. He just put on an apron and started washing dishes like he'd never left.

Tomas was like a cult hero; all the regular bar customers knew him. One time when he came back from one of his family visits, my father handed him a broom and told him to sweep the sidewalk. Two hours later, one of the regulars came into the bar and told us he was glad to see Tomas was back. When asked how he knew the dishwasher had returned, the guest said he saw Tomas sweeping the sidewalk on Sixth Street. The Redwood was on First Street. My father sent one of the other dishwashers to retrieve Tomas. I think if he had not been stopped, he would have swept every sidewalk in downtown LA.

One of the many lessons I learned from my father was about loyalty. A liquor salesman convinced me to change the vodka brand in the bar. Vodka was the number one selling liquor. I bought 10 cases at a special price. When the product came in, my father asked where it came from. I explained I bought it for a lower price from a different company than the one he normally used.

"How much did you save?" he asked. "Fifty dollars," I replied.

Then, he calmly asked me if our 10-year relationship with the other company was worth $50? He also told me our regular company allowed 90 days to pay for the merchandise when we were short of cash. "How do you think it would look if they came in and saw we were pouring someone else's vodka? The loyalty I've shown this company has kept me in business."

I knew my dad wasn't mad at me, he just wanted me to learn a very valuable lesson, one that stayed with me for the rest of my career. Later, when we opened our restaurants, my motto was, *"We take care of our guests, our team members, our purveyors, and the rest takes care of itself."*

Another group of regular bar customers came from the California Attorney General's office. They were smart, had exciting jobs, and were also big drinkers. Several of them were very involved in Democratic politics, which appealed to me as well, and I became friends with many of them. One of those friends was Jerry Brown, whose father was governor of California. I grew to know him and even worked on his successful campaign for governor of California. In later years, several of my attorney general friends became judges. I've maintained these friendships for over 40 years.

Another regular guest at the Redwood was Phil Montez, the executive director of the Western Regional Office of the United States Commission on Civil Rights. I was very interested in civil rights and Phil and I became good friends. He introduced me to many of the politicians he worked with. I was so interested in the subject that Phil nominated me for an appointment to the Commission. My name was given to President Lyndon

Johnson, and I was appointed in 1965. We held hearings around the state in underserved communities that needed our support to get re-development funds, better schools, and jobs to their communities. It was heart-breaking to hear some of their stories but quite rewarding when we could help. We also lobbied congress members to help these communities.

Throughout this time, Beth and I were serious about each other. I felt that her parents, who were better educated and more cultured than mine, were seriously concerned that their daughter was dating someone who did not go on to college. My father was the saving grace. Beth's parents recognized that he seemed to have a very successful business and therefore, my financial future looked good, despite my limited education. Even though they felt that way, it was still quite a conflict — for them.

In 1966, Beth and I decided to get married. We had a beautiful wedding in my father's and Rosemary's back yard. Don, who had thrown baseballs at my head 10 years before, was best man. After the wedding, we spent the night at the Beverly Hilton hotel in Beverly Hills and then went on to Mexico for a honeymoon. Then I went back to work at the Redwood. By this time, I was totally capable of running the entire restaurant and my father started taking more time off.

On December 12, 1966, my son Jason was born. This beautiful, six-pound, blue-eyed baby changed my life. I never worried about anyone like I did for Jason. When Jason was about 3 years old and running a fever, Beth and I naively thought we needed to wrap him in a wool blanket. We found out later that was *exactly* the wrong thing to do. Jason went into fever convulsions.

We called the pediatrician, Buddy Zukow, and he rushed over to our house. I have never been as scared as I was then.

Even at 3 years old, we could tell Jason was very smart, and I prayed we didn't do permanent damage to him by wrapping him in that warm blanket.

When Buddy arrived, he assured us Jason was going to be OK. I knew my life was never going to be the same. I was responsible for this little life!

I worked at the Redwood for three years. My father taught me everything there was to know about running the restaurant and about people. When Beth and I started having children, I felt it was time to start thinking about opening my own business.

I came up with the idea of opening a takeout and delivery restaurant in Tarzana named Smokey Joe's Pony Express. The idea was to serve the most popular items from the Smokey Joe's menu: BBQ Beef, Turkey and Ham sandwiches, BBQ spareribs, and BBQ chicken. This was a great idea but I made one fatal error.

Microwave ovens had just come on the market. Dad and I were dazzled by the fact that you could heat the sandwich in a paper bag without the paper getting burnt or even hot. This seemed like a miracle. We were so blinded by the equipment that we failed to realize what it did to the French Roll. The microwave made bread very soft and chewy until it cooled off, at which time the bread turned hard as a rock. I don't think the restaurant lasted a year.

By this time, it was 1970 and Beth and I had our second miracle, a baby girl named Elissa Sari. She was a beautiful little girl and the light of my life. Having a daughter is a totally different experience. When that little girl looks into your eyes and calls you "Daddy," it's a feeling that can't be described. (Elissa still calls me Daddy.)

Now I had two children and my first major business failure.

I went back to work for my dad.

By this time, his business was in serious financial difficulty. I didn't know it, but all these years he had "borrowed from Peter to pay Paul." He had not paid the restaurants' withholding taxes to the IRS for several months and owed $10,000. The IRS caught up with him nine months later.

I went to his apartment the morning the IRS had designated as the deadline to pay the money. My dad didn't have it. This had been going on for several years and he had run out of friends to loan him the money. When I walked into his apartment, my father was as pale as a ghost and suffering from serious chest pains. It was obvious he was very sick and I told Rosemary to call an ambulance. When the ambulance arrived, they rushed him to the hospital. He was having a heart attack. I called the IRS and explained what had happened. After they called the hospital to verify my story, they gave me one month to pay the taxes.

My dad survived the heart attack and I was able to raise the money to pay the IRS and keep the restaurants going. Since he was sick and not spending any money, I was able to straighten out the restaurant finances. But once he started feeling better, the spending picked up, and I realized the restaurant couldn't support both of us.

I told him the Redwood was his restaurant and I was going to have to let him come back to run it. I would find another job. He decided that he didn't want to continue to run it without me and closed the restaurant in the early 1970s. There was just enough money to pay his bills and get out of the business, but that was all. Meanwhile, I was 27 with a wife, two children, a mortgage, and I was out of work.

Chapter 5
Making My Way

My mother played cards with Serrette Gettleman. Her husband, Maurie, owned the Foods concession in Fedco, a membership store much like Costco. I started working at the deli counter selling sliced meats, salads, lox and bagels, etc. I worked long hours, six days a week, and did everything asked of me. Maurie had a daughter and a son working with the company and I got along with them very well. Whenever Mr. G (as we would call him) would come to the location where I was working, he always took the time to sit down and talk to me. He was interested in my thoughts on what Corporate could do to improve the prepared foods department and he wanted to know more about my restaurant background. I was about the only one he would stop and talk to. One time, my manager was cleaning out the peanut butter machine. Nobody liked that messy job. When I offered to do it, he said, "Thanks, but it's all in a day's work." Even though he was the manager, it wasn't beneath him to clean the machine by himself. I never forgot those words. Throughout my restaurant career I told people that whatever job they were given, just remember, *"It's all in a day's work."*

Within six months I was the manager of the Foods department and later became responsible for all six Foods departments for the Fedco stores.

In 1976, when I had been with Fedco for about five years, Mr. G came to me with the idea of opening a soup-and-salad buffet restaurant. He knew I had restaurant experience and came to talk with me about his idea. I liked the idea and he asked me if I would transfer from Fedco Foods to help him open Soup 'n Such. Of course, I was very excited and said yes without even talking to Beth. When I called and told her, she was excited as this was an advancement in my career.

Soup 'n Such would have 31 different soups and feature four soups a day, along with several salads, all arranged in a buffet line. Maurie had a company named IBM Foods which cooked all the prepared foods for Fedco and prepared meals for most of the airlines. They developed all the soup recipes and I ran the restaurant. If you asked Maurie what IBM stood for he would tell you, "It Belongs to Maurie."

We opened the first Soup 'n Such on Bedford Drive in Beverly Hills. The second one opened on Weyburn Avenue in Westwood. We would cook the soups at the Beverly Hills location and I would pick them up and drive them about three miles to the Westwood store. They would fill 12 white, 3-gallon plastic buckets with the soup and load them into the back of my Ford Station Wagon.

One day while delivering the soups down Wilshire Boulevard, a car swerved in front of me and I jammed on the brakes. The soup rushed forward, the lids of all 12 buckets popped off and I was hit in the back of my neck with 36 gallons of hot Boston Clam Chowder! The inside of the windshield was covered with so much milky chowder I couldn't see out the front, so I turned off Wilshire onto a side street and parked in front of a private house. I got out of the car and used my hands to sweep the clams, potatoes, and cream soup onto the lawn. I often wonder what the owner of the house thought when they saw that white, creamy mess on his green lawn!

Now that I could somewhat see out the windshield, I drove to the Westwood restaurant with the remaining soup that was still in the buckets. The kitchen team helped me clean the car as best we could and then I went home, quite dejected.

When I got home, Jason and Elissa couldn't believe how I looked; clam chowder was splotched over my clothes and I even had clams in the pocket of my jacket. I don't believe I've eaten Boston clam chowder since that day.

I worked at Soup 'n Such for about two years when we decided to open a third location on Wilshire Boulevard in the mid-Wilshire district two blocks east of La Cienega Boulevard in Los Angeles. The first two restaurants did well, but not great. The third one did not do well at all. By this time, it was 1977 and I realized all my hard work was not getting me very far.

Marshall Fischer, the owner of Office Construction Co. that built our third restaurant, offered me a job with his construction company. His company built the interiors of large office buildings and he wanted to get into building restaurants. Marshall thought I could help him do that. I was working so hard at Soup 'n Such and could see it wasn't going anywhere and Beth was fed up with my hours and not having enough money to live the way we wanted to. Marshall not only offered me a job, he told me I could drive his Rolls Royce Corniche Convertible, or his Ferrari, or his four-door 600 Mercedes and I would have a credit card with an unlimited expense account for anything that could be considered a business expense. He also offered me $15,000 a year more than I was making at the restaurant, with regular working hours from nine to five. How could I do anything but say yes? And so, I went to work for him.

Telling Maurie I was leaving was very difficult for me. Our relationship was almost like a father-son. I did, and always have, considered him to be my mentor. He taught me about handling food, controlling costs, and above all, how to be stern but fair. Later when I was opening The Grill restaurants, I took Maurie through the restaurant and got his blessing. He was quite a man and I will never forget him. He passed away several years ago and the family asked me to give the eulogy at his funeral.

One of the additional benefits of the new job was that I had time to coach Jason's Encino Little League team, an experience that would bring unexpected benefits later.

Encino Baseball California League Expos – Photo Day 1979. Backrow: Bob Spivak, Manager (adult in the middle), Jason Spivak, #12 at right. Front Row: Eric Garcetti #16 (middle) and my friend Don Calabria's twins are #4 and #5.

Jason was 10 years old and this was his first year of Little League. I needed an assistant coach and one of the fathers, Jack Gilardi, volunteered. Before I agreed to have him help me, I wanted to let him know my philosophy of coaching these young kids. I let him know we were there to teach the kids how to play baseball, be good sports, good teammates, and have a good time. If we won some games, that was all the better. More importantly, I wanted the kids to have a good experience and enjoy the game. Jack agreed and we became a great coaching team and close friends.

Jack was a talent agent with International Creative Management, one of the largest talent agencies in Hollywood, and he represented several big stars of the times like Jaclyn Smith ("Charlie's Angels"), Telly Savalas ("Kojak"), Frankie Avalon, Ann Margret, and O.J. Simpson. At the end of every Little League season, we would hold a fund-raising event with all Jack's clients entertaining the guests. Jack was married to Annette Funicello, and she would perform at the events as well.

Eric Garcetti, who became mayor of Los Angeles in 2014 and is currently the United States Ambassador to India, was on one of my Little League teams. I was a big supporter of Eric's and heard many of his speeches. No matter how large the crowd, when he caught my eye in the audience, he would stop speaking and come down from the stage, give me a hug and a kiss, then go right back on the stage and let the crowd know that I was his coach.

One time I was in a meeting with Eric and about 20 other people around a large oval table while he was Mayor. We all introduced ourselves. I let the group know I was Eric's Little League coach and then proceeded to tell them how lucky they were that Eric was a better mayor than a ball player. He interrupted to let me and the group know he hit .400 that year. This was a very high batting average. The last person in the major leagues to achieve this was Ted Williams in the 1940s. I said, "Yes, but he still is a better mayor."

Bob and Leslie Spivak with Los Angeles Mayor Eric Garcetti at the Mayor's house, 2016

I coached my son Jason for two seasons and then coached my daughter Elissa for two additional seasons. Not only was it a great bonding experience with my children but I also met a lot of people who are still my friends to this day. One of the fathers I met was Mike Weinstock who would later become one of my business partners.

When Jason was 12 years old, some of the coaches put together a team to go to Taiwan and play against the Taiwanese Little League teams. Jason went on the trip and had a great experience, even though the American kids were unable to compete at the level of players in Taiwan. One team was so good they brought in 7-year-old players to allow the American kids to get the Taiwan team out.

The job with Marshall Fischer only lasted one year. I was like a fish out of water in the construction business. So now I was 36 years old with a wife, two children, a mortgage on our house in Encino, and unemployed.

My mother's cousin, Paul Garett, owned a 500-acre organic vegetable ranch in Santa Barbara, California. I went to work with Paul to help him market the vegetables. Paul was an eccentric person who would go to auctions and buy old farming equipment. Nothing that we needed; he just couldn't bear to see good, but obsolete, equipment go to waste. Part of my job was to sell the old equipment Paul bought — and I mean old. Some of the equipment was over 100 years old and used back when all the farming was done with horses.

Each weekend I would drive one of the old trucks to the farmers markets in Los Angeles and sell the organic produce. I brought Jason with me and he did most of the selling. He was so cute and articulate the customers couldn't say no to him. Between marketing the produce, selling old equipment, and driving 150 miles a day from Encino to Santa Barbara and back home, I was again out of my element and that job also lasted one year.

Jason Spivak, 12, bagging tomatoes at the Los Angeles Farmers Market, 1980

Now I'm 37, out of work, with a wife, two children, and a mortgage. I tried another job —selling solar pool heaters on commission. I wasn't very good at that either.

Through all of this, my marriage was feeling the pressure. Beth and I still loved each other but the financial struggle and the uncertainty of a career along with 70- and 80-hour work weeks put a lot of stress on our marriage. When I was 38 and she was 35, we agreed it was time to split up and go our separate ways.

I moved in with my father and Rosemary because I didn't have enough money to take care of Beth *and* the kids and have my own apartment. I was still selling solar pool heaters and made just enough commission to keep Beth and the kids going. This was the lowest point of my life.

Then, Mike Weinstock, whose son had been on my Little League team, called. While attending his twentieth high school reunion, he talked to a classmate, Richard Shapiro, whom I also knew. Both men were financially successful and shared an interest in opening a restaurant. During their discussion, my name came up as a person they both knew and liked who had extensive restaurant experience. They called and we decided to meet for lunch at the Bel-Air Sands hotel in Brentwood on Tuesday, February 9, 1982—the day that would change my life, professionally and personally.

Chapter 6
Turning Point

Bel-Air Sands Hotel – Brentwood, CA
Tuesday, February 9, 1982

I suppose it was only natural that I had ideas for a restaurant. Anyone who's ever worked in the food service industry has entertained thoughts of "If this was *my* restaurant, I'd do it *this* way." But having ideas and implementing them were two different things and I'd never given those ideas much thought. Until now.

"I want to open a traditional American Grill," I said. This concept bucked the current California Cuisine trends of nouvelle cuisine, fusion cooking, and small portions with artistic presentations. Mike and Richard ate their lunches as I explained. "Like the Tadich Grill, Jack's, Sam's Grill in San Francisco, and Musso & Frank in Hollywood."

These restaurants had several things in common: they had been around since the 1930s, were run by several generations of families, and served top-quality food. They all had large "daily dated" menus offering over 80 choices of food dishes, with items made fresh every day.

"Our restaurant will be straight forward. Honest." I continued. "The food will be the best quality available with very few sauces." (Some restaurants used sauces to disguise poor food quality.) "We'll find a high-visibility location in a trendy area, like Beverly Hills."

The 1980s was a time of great pretense in the LA restaurant scene. Michaels in Santa Monica was a fine restaurant and still is to this day. At Michaels, there were no substitutions. You ate the food the way the chef prepared it, or you didn't eat at all. If you asked for a salad with the dressing on the side, the chef might come out and tell you he only serves it tossed with the dressing.

Ma Maison, a restaurant in West Hollywood that catered to celebrities, had an unlisted phone number. You couldn't call for a reservation unless you knew someone who had the number. The food was excellent; Wolfgang Puck was the Executive chef. But if you weren't on the A-List, chances are you wouldn't get near Puck's chicken with whole grain mustard sauce.

Our restaurant would be just the opposite. If you had a reservation, we would honor it whether your name was Frank Sinatra or Frank Smith. "At this restaurant, the guest is always right and the answer is 'yes – what is the question?'"

Richard and Mike liked the sound of this and by the end of the lunch, we shook hands on a deal. The three of us would be equal partners and work together. Richard and Mike would focus on the design and fundraising. They would pay me a small salary to find a location. The three of us would develop the concept including menu, food preparation, and service. However, I wouldn't get my one-third ownership until all the investors were paid back. We planned to repay the investment in 36 months. (In fact, we exceeded expectations and were able to repay the investors within 16 months, and my ownership became vested.)

Now remember, at this time I was getting a divorce after 16 years of marriage and living at my father's house because I didn't have enough income to take care of Beth, Jason and Elissa, and still afford my own apartment. My funds were so low, Richard had to take me out and buy two suits for me to wear when working at the restaurant. I'd had three jobs in three years — the latest selling solar pool heaters — and wasn't very successful at any of them. But I kept at it because I still had a family to support and that was my priority.

After we'd reached our agreement, I rose from the table to go make a phone call. I wanted to tell my father about the meeting. As I walked through the dining room toward the back where the payphones were located, a pretty blonde woman stopped me.

"Aren't you Bobby Spivak?"

It was Leslie Martin, the girl I had a crush on in junior high school! We exchanged some pleasantries, I made my phone call, then went back to my table. It turned out that both Mike and Richard also knew Leslie, so when we were ready to leave, the three of us walked over and talked to Leslie and her friend, who was also a classmate of ours.

Richard and Mike said their goodbyes and after Leslie's friend left, it was just the two of us. We talked about a lot of things while I tried to get her phone number. She told me she and her sister, Linda, were making hors d'oeuvres to sell to takeout restaurants and kitchen stores. They made the food in Linda's home but realized they needed a professional kitchen to work in. *This was my opening.* My father now had a small restaurant named Bouillabaisse that was only open for dinner.

"Maybe you can use my father's kitchen during the day," I told her, knowing very well that my father wouldn't let *anyone* use his kitchen. The ruse worked and I got Leslie's phone number. I called a few days later to meet Leslie for a drink. We met at 7 p.m. at the Corkscrew, a restaurant on San Vicente Boulevard in Brentwood. We sat in the bar and talked about everything—except the kitchen.

Leslie had two children; a boy, Todd, who was 16, and a daughter, Dayna, who was 13. She and her husband were separated. I told her my son Jason was 13 and my daughter Elissa was 11. I'm not sure how we filled up three hours, but we did. We each had one drink and at 10 p.m. the server came over and said the restaurant was closing; we had to leave. As we walked out the door, I asked if she wanted to take a ride. She said yes.

We drove to Sorrento Beach in Santa Monica, which is where any Van Nuys High School boy would take a date. I parked in the lot, and we continued to talk while Simon and Garfunkel's double cassette tape of *The Concert in Central Park* played three complete revolutions. We talked about growing up in the San Fernando Valley, going to Van Nuys Jr. High School, politics, and everything in between. Before we knew it, it was 3 a.m. I told Leslie I had to call my friend Helen Bernstein and tell her about the night.

"You can't call anyone at three in the morning," Leslie said. "I can call Helen," I told her.

Helen and I met years ago when she tutored Beth at UCLA. Helen's boyfriend, Harvey, was looking for a place to live and there was an extra room where I lived so Harvey moved in. Later, as married couples, we became good friends, but only Helen and I retained a friendship after our respective marriages ended. Helen was my closest friend and the only person I *could* call at 3 a.m.

We drove around looking for a pay phone (cell phones had not been invented yet) and found one at Palisades Park. I didn't have any change to make the phone call so Leslie gave me a dime and I called Helen.

Of course, at 3 a.m. in the morning, I woke her up. My exact words were, "Helen, I'm in love."

She said, "Bob, it's three in the morning." "Yes, I know.

When I started to explain, she asked, "Bob, is this relationship going to last until seven in the morning?"

"Yes," I answered.

"Good. Call me then." She hung up the phone.

Leslie and I are married now and have been together since that night over 40 years ago. We are rarely apart. The success I had going forward was due, in large part, to Leslie. She is definitely the "blonde" who saved me.

Leslie Martin at the Beverly Hills Hotel and Bobby Spivak at a track meet, 1960

Chapter 7
Creating the Concept

Richard, Mike, and I set out to give life to the concept. We went to Musso & Frank in Hollywood and the Pacific Dining Car in downtown Los Angeles. We flew to San Francisco to study the Tadich Grill, Jack's Grill, and Sam's Grill, all restaurants which were built in the 1920s and 1930s and had been doing things the same way since the day they opened.

The Tadich Grill which was the best known of all the grills in San Francisco. We studied everything about it. The tabletops were simple but impeccable and covered with white tablecloths. The napkins were starched white cloth napkins made of 100% cotton—no polyester—and had to be ironed after each washing. (Cotton napkins were more absorbent than poly blend napkins.) They used silver-plated flatware rather than stainless steel. The salt and pepper shakers were glass with silver tops and were the only items on the table. The menus were typeset (not computerized) and printed daily with the current date including the year, sending the subliminal message that all the food was prepared special that day. The food portions were large, served on heavy off-white china plates, and garnished with a small piece of parsley. The servers all wore white "waiters coats" over a starched white dress shirt, black ironed slacks, and black shoes.

These restaurants all had common threads of our Traditional American Grill concept: large menus, fresh ingredients, tables laid with white tablecloths, cloth napkins, heavy place settings, and servers' uniforms embroidered with the restaurant's name. These kinds of details whispered *elegance* without distracting from the food, which was the real star.

63

Leslie, Richard, Mike, and I also flew to New York City to check out the bars. Leslie and I visited 56 bars in five days. While we weren't planning on opening a restaurant in New York, we wanted to experience the energy and the atmosphere.

Our approach was to go in each establishment as customers. We took mental rather than written notes and then later discussed our experiences; what we liked, didn't like, and what features they all had in common that comprised a traditional New York bar.

We noticed all the bottles were stacked three rows high behind the bar and the bar surfaces held only liquor bottles and glasses. None of the establishments had electric blenders; the mixed drinks were vigorously shaken by male bartenders who all seemed to possess the "gift of gab."

We incorporated these traits in our concept. Paying attention to details like these didn't go unnoticed as later, many people commented how much The Grill on the Alley "felt" like a New York restaurant.

"Concept" is a broad term that covers numerous aspects of the business. First, there's the type of restaurant: fast food, quick service, full service, casual dining, median-priced full service and fine dining. From there, you need to choose what type of food and beverages to serve, menu options, table settings, and how to train and present the servers. It's a puzzle that, once complete, fulfills a vision.

Even as we worked out the details of our concept, I was searching for the right location for our American grill. Richard and Mike would check out each possible site with me but there always seemed to be some reason why a location wouldn't work.

There are so many variables to finding the right location. You have to consider parking, visibility, signage potential, size and configuration of interior space, height of ceiling, and of course, the occupancy cost which includes rent, real estate taxes, maintenance, and common area maintenance charges. There is a formula for rent based on how many seats you can comfortably fit into the space versus the occupancy cost. After you total all those charges, you need to estimate the number of sales a location will generate.

One of the key variables is figuring out how much business you would do and how many meal periods you will be able to open. The most consistent lunch traffic comes from office buildings because people are there Monday through Friday. For dinner you want to have a dense residential population. Apartments are important because there are more people living in a smaller area than if there were single-family homes. Then on the weekends, you had to consider if there was enough shopping nearby to support lunch traffic and were there enough evening activities, such as movie theaters, to attract customers. All these factors come into play in defining a "good" location.

Finally, after about four months of searching, I walked past Tokyo, a defunct Sushi bar at 9561 Wilshire Boulevard in Beverly Hills. The front door faced Wilshire Boulevard, one of the city's main arteries. The front door was locked but an index card taped to the door read, "For information on this building call…" and a phone number.

I walked around to the back of the building and found a fire exit door leading from the bar to the alley that opened on Dayton Way. If we could make the alley our main entrance, this could be the place we'd been looking for. I immediately called Richard and Mike. After seeing the location, we were all in agreement; this was the place!

I called the number, spoke to the owner, and made an appointment to meet him in his office. Mr. Horton was a cordial older man and I got along with him quite well. I told him what we wanted to do with the entrance off the alley and we worked out a one-month option. There was nothing to the interior of the building, just four walls and an area where the Sushi kitchen had been. It was like an empty table, waiting to be set.

The next day I went to the Beverly Hills Planning Department. When I explained that I wanted to use the alley door as the main entrance to the restaurant, they said there was NO WAY they would approve the front door opening into an active alley.

I went home and called Mike and Richard with the news. Despite the emphatic rebuke, we all agreed it was worth pursuing as we felt the alley entrance was the most important element of the building for several reasons.

The view of the alley entrance at The Grill on the Alley with Giorgio building at left.

The corner of Dayton Way and Rodeo Drive is one of the most famous corners in the world. The alley door put us next door to Giorgio, the luxury fragrance boutique. Also, there was no stopping along Wilshire Boulevard, therefore, valet parking was out of the question if the front door faced Wilshire. Most importantly, that entrance made us different: an unpretentious and off-the-beaten-path entryway to a different dining experience.

I gave a lot of thought to the alley entrance and was set on figuring out a way to turn No into a Yes, much like I did in my school years to find the "angle" necessary to get the outcome I wanted. The first thing I did was go back to the building department and pull the plot plan for the restaurant building. I was in luck; the back of the building had an inch of frontage on Dayton Way before it went down the alley. This gave me an idea.

Channeling my father and our grocery store schemes, I went to the hardware store and bought a mailbox, the kind you might find on the front door of a small house. Next, I needed a new address. The Artistic Shoe Repair store next door to the restaurant was 9562 so I invented the address of 9560 Dayton Way.

I painted the address on my mailbox and hung it on the inch of frontage. Then I went to the post office and mailed a letter to myself at 9560 Dayton Way. Two days later, my letter was delivered. I took the letter with the cancelled stamp to the building department, showed them that the address did indeed exist, and obtained approval to use the alley door as the main entrance since now it was technically on Dayton Way. Today, we have a brass plaque at that exact corner adjacent to our one-inch of frontage that reads "THE GRILL."

The Grill on The Alley – Beverly Hills, CA

Now for the big problem: money. We figured it would take about $650,000 to open the doors. That included everything from remodeling the space to hiring and training staff.

First, we needed an architect. We hired Iden Zaima who had designed the Soups 'n Such restaurants for me and Maurie Gettleman in 1980. I was familiar with his work and knew he would be a good fit for the restaurant. Iden did a floor plan for the space that included the locations for the kitchen, bar, booths, tables and chairs, and service stations we could use to help describe the restaurant to potential investors. We hired Steve Reiman, a well-known interior designer, who we felt would complement Iden's architectural design.

Steve created a design similar to those classic steakhouses of the past but with modern details. The ceiling, painted white to reflect light, had a series of coffers with stacked moldings which created an acoustical oasis allowing for private conversations amongst the buzzing of a busy restaurant. While the ceilings were a major expense, they allowed us to have a packed room with great energy where guests could actually talk to one another.

The main lighting consisted of two massive, antique brass chandeliers in the center of the room. Each chandelier had eight brass arms and each arm held a glass globe. Wall sconces throughout the booth and table seating areas exuded a warm glow which was magnified by glass mirrors that extended from chair-rail height of the seating areas to the ceiling. The flooring was white marble squares accented with smaller black squares.

The dining room had 13 booths and 20 tables. The booths, separated by frosted glass partitions, created a sense of privacy without confinement and the seats were covered in green leather. The booths provided a semiprivate space for business meetings as well as parties of four dining together. I'm convinced that our booths were a major draw for dealmakers throughout the decades: like the Seinfeld deal that was both penned and celebrated here in booth 106. People didn't have to shout at one another to be heard. The one exception that comes to mind was the nonstop, uproarious laughter and loud singing from table 105 when Mel Brooks and Anne Bancroft and Carl and Estelle Reiner invited Carole Burnett and her choreographer, who had been sitting in adjacent booth 106, to join them. Our acoustics, thankfully, couldn't muffle that dinner party!

The tables provided a great deal of versatility. There were small tables for two and larger tables for parties of four people. All the four-tops had flip-up rounded ends which could accommodate up to eight guests when opened. Each table would be set with a sterling silver vase containing a single red carnation. All these elements created an atmosphere of accessible elegance, exactly what we had in mind.

I had searched for a Chef for about three months before I interviewed John Sola. At the time, he was 28 years old and the Chef at The Chronicle in Santa Monica where he worked for his mentor, Rolf Nonnast. Rolf was a classically trained German chef at Scandia and was renowned for his recipes and attention to detail. Scandia was one of the three most famous restaurants in Los Angeles in the 1960s and 1970s and a great background for our future chef.

Richard, Mike, Leslie and I went to The Chronicle for dinner to taste John's food and watch him work. I could tell right away that John had a good attitude by the way the servers and cooks talked about him, and to me, a good attitude was almost as important as actual cooking skills. John had learned to emphasize cooking that allowed fresh ingredients to speak for themselves and was recognized as a "Rising Star of American Cuisine" by the James Beard Foundation. I knew that potential investors would be impressed.

A great chef has to be not only an excellent cook but also an excellent businessperson as they are responsible for: the cost of goods sold, labor cost, storing of food, freshness of produce, purchasing, cleanliness etc. John had all the skills. He was demanding (and yes, in the beginning everyone was scared to death of Sola...he had this look that would make cooks and servers alike stop and cry) but he was well-respected and highly regarded by all.

After hiring John Sola, I wanted to show him what we were trying to achieve at The Grill, so Leslie and I took him to San Francisco to several of the "Traditional American Grills" that we had visited earlier. When we returned to Los Angeles, we went to Musso and Frank in Hollywood. John now understood the understated "less is more" vision we had for the American Grill that Mike, Richard, and I had discussed the day we became partners.

Now it was time to work on the food. John, Leslie, and I spent the entire year working on the menu. We would meet at my apartment once a week. John and I would cook, Leslie did the dishes, and we all tasted the food. Almost without exception, every dish John made was a success. After we felt we got it right, we would have a tasting with Richard and Mike.

We arranged a cocktail party at the Beverly Wilshire hotel to present our concept using Iden's drawings and showcasing my expertise in the restaurant business. Chef John Sola prepared the hors d'oeuvres and we provided a sample menu. Some of the specialty items on the menu included:

Entrees:

    Braised Short Ribs
    Calves Liver Bordelaise
    Steak Tartare
    Prime Rib Hash
    Veal Marsala
    Veal Piccata
    Dungeness Crab Cakes
    Pan Fried Fish
    Bay Scallops
    Chicken Pot Pie

Soups:

    Navy Bean
    Mushroom Barley
    Manhattan Clam Chowder
    Split Pea with Smokes Ham Hocks
    Lentil with sausage
    Crab and Corn Chowder

Salads:

> Caesar with broiled Chicken
> Shrimp Louie
> Crab Louie
> Rare Ahi Tuna
> Niçoise salad with Ahi Tuna

Mike and Richard knew people who might be interested in investing in a restaurant. I didn't have any contacts; therefore, they were 100 percent responsible for raising the money. After about four months of intense work, including more parties, meetings, and phone calls, we were able to raise the entire $650,000. Some of the "high visibility" investors were Grant Tinker (former NBC CEO and ex-husband of Mary Tyler Moore), Peter Horton (director and actor of hit television show "Thirtysomething"), and award-winning actress Michelle Pfeiffer.

***

Six months before hiring John Sola, my dad came to me and said he was going to open another restaurant. It was going to serve one entrée: Bouillabaisse. When I was growing up, my dad would make Bouillabaisse for his friends. It tasted like fish stew to me, but his friends loved it! He went on to tell me he and Rosemary would bring all their china dishes and silver from home and use it for the service.

At the time, my dad was 66 years old and had been working for Lawry's restaurants for the past eight years. I pleaded with him not to open the restaurant; he was too old to launch something new and not in the best of health. I also told him he was only two years away from being fully vested in Lawry's retirement program and not to give that up. His answer to me was, "If the Kentucky Colonel can start a business at age 66, I can too."

My dad didn't have any money at all. But I'll be damned if he didn't get the Bouillabaisse open! He found a location on the third floor of an office building in Encino which had been Howard Hughes' private suite of offices. It had two small rooms with plush green carpeting, heavy crown molding, beautiful green and white wallpaper, and a small kitchen that would work with his very limited menu (the same kitchen I had offered up to Leslie in order to get her phone number). He then went to an antique furniture dealer and talked the owner into giving him 10 antique wood tables and 40 chairs for 10 percent ownership in the restaurant. Five tables and 20 chairs just fit into each of the two rooms. He borrowed $5,000 from a friend, and he was off and running.

Now, this is normally not the way to open a restaurant, and really, my dad couldn't afford this venture. But with a little luck and creativity he prevailed. Luck that he found a space that was ready to go and creative in the sense of negotiating a deal with the antique dealer providing the furniture and also using their personal serving dishes and silverware rather than purchasing brand new.

The restaurant seated 40 people and was open Wednesday, Thursday, Friday, and Saturday nights for one seating at 7 p.m. They served a special mixed green salad, the Bouillabaisse with a homemade rouille (made with wine vinegar, saffron, lots of garlic, egg yolks, chili powder and olive oil), fresh-baked French Bread, and a piece of lemon dipped in dark chocolate and Lemon Sorbet or Chocolate Mousse Cake for dessert.

You either came at 7 p.m. and ate Bouillabaisse or you didn't come at all. If someone asked for bread when the salads were being served, Rosemary would tell the guest, "You don't get bread until the Bouillabaisse is served because I don't want you to fill up on the bread."

Creating the Concept

My dad needed a chef and I loaned him John Sola as we hadn't yet opened The Grill. This did two things for me. First, I was able to learn more about John's attitude toward the team members, his work ethic and cooking ability. It also allowed me to hire John for The Grill one year before we opened and work with him one day a week developing the menu. It was a win-win for all of us.

For entertainment, my dad and Rosemary hired a Flamenco guitar player. The music started slow and mellow and then as the night went on, would speed up the tempos so that by the end of the evening the servers were dancing an Irish jig and the place broke out into one big party. The restaurant became so popular that it took three to four weeks to get a reservation.

The Bouillabaisse was a runaway hit. My Dad and Rosemary fulfilled their lifelong dream of owning and operating their own restaurant together, although it only lasted from 1980 to 1985. My dad was in the kitchen and Rosemary was the host. My father would come out of the kitchen with his apron on to greet guests and share his wealth of stories. It was like going to their house for a fabulous dinner party. They brought together a crew of five women who were both servers and the dancers. This special group became my father and Rosemary's family, and that sense of family extended to their guests. People today still tell me they remember the Bouillabaisse.

My father had a massive stroke and was unable to continue operating the Bouillabaisse. It was definitely the end of an era and I felt the responsibility to be successful and carry the Spivak name to the next generation of Restaurateurs.

***

All this time that my dad and Rosemary were running Bouillabaisse, we were building The Grill and hiring and training the team.

74

Leslie, John Sola and I went to the National Restaurant Show in Chicago and met with many of the purveyors. This is where we met with Homer Laughlin fine china and picked out the dish pattern: Green Band with rolled edges which would make it easier for servers to grasp. We also picked out Oneida Old English silver-plate flatware, along with tabletop accessories, uniforms, tables, and chairs. Richard and Mike did an excellent job of choosing wall sconces, chandeliers, and bathroom fixtures that were traditional and unpretentious.

We hired a kitchen designer named Tony Singuas who, along with John Sola, was responsible for all the cooking equipment. Carolyn Vineyard, a wine consultant who had consulted with my father and Rosemary on the wine list at the Bouillabaisse, was hired to choose our wines.

In 1983, Mimi Sheraton, a food critic and writer for the New York Times magazine, wrote a story about a French Bistro in Paris, L'Ami Louis. Chef Antoine Magnin, who cooked for the original Louis, could still be found behind the oak-fired charcoal broiler in full view of the dining room where the guests could watch their meals being cooked.

At this time of my life, the thought of ever going to Paris was out of the question. However, Mimi painted such a vivid picture of L'Ami Louis that it inspired me: our American Grill foods would be cooked on an oak-fired broiler that would also be visible to our guests.

Working with Steve Bernstein at Jade Range Cooking Equipment, we designed a custom barbeque broiler which burned Oak charcoal, the hottest of all the wood charcoals. (Most people order steaks rare or medium rare, and when cooking the meat, you want to char the outside while still achieving the rare or medium rare temperature inside. Using the hotter burning charcoal accomplishes this.) We added

Hickory wood chips to give the meat a smokey taste.

Rick Nicholas, who owned Newport Meat Company, handpicked all our protein; we used only Prime meats. His company supports local farms and ranches producing natural and sustainable meats. He, along with John Sola and myself, were responsible for procuring only the finest food products.

Our purchasing philosophy was to be fair with our purveyors and pay them early. If we sent something back because the quality was not up to our specifications, they knew we meant business. Our goal was to be *their* best customer. That way, they couldn't afford to take any chances with our business. After all, the most important element was the food.

Musso and Frank used a printer who used the old letterpress method of setting individual letters and lines of type to make their daily menus. I found the name of the print shop and contacted Gil, the owner, to see if he would print our menus the same way. He laughed and told me he had several people who wanted to copy their menu over the years, and nobody had ever followed through. When we ordered the first week of daily dated menus, Gil knew I was serious. Sometimes the o's had a little ink in the middle which often happened in the printing process, harkening back to days past, which made even the menu seem special. (Later on, he not only printed all our lunch and dinner menus, he printed *all* the menus for the Daily Grill as well.) We became his biggest customer, by far.

Chapter 8
The Food is The Star

The Grill's menu grew to include hearty all-American daily soups, Cobb salad, Chicken Pot Pie, and Rice Pudding.

One of our more popular items was the Cobb salad, which is perhaps the most famous as well as the most misrepresented salad on menus across America. Most people think a Cobb salad is the same as a chopped salad—it's not. Here's the story.

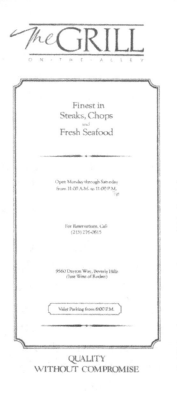

The Grill on the Alley menu cover, 1984

The Food is The Star

The Brown Derby, a famous restaurant in Beverly Hills, was owned by a man named Bob Cobb. One night Bob walked into his bar. It was late and the kitchen had closed but there were several people sitting at the bar and they were hungry; they wanted to order food. So, Mr. Cobb went to the kitchen to see what he could do. The only food ingredients that weren't locked up were: finely chopped chives, blue cheese crumbles, cooked diced chicken, bacon crumbles, peeled and quartered hard boiled eggs, coarsely chopped romaine lettuce, and halved cherry tomatoes. Mr. Cobb put all the ingredients together, tossed them with a creamy vinaigrette dressing, and brought it out to the bar.

The next night, Bob again dropped by the bar late in the evening. "Hey Bob," one of his customers said, "make us another one of those Cobb salads." And that's how the Cobb salad was born. We recreated that salad exactly as Mr. Cobb made it and it became a signature dish for The Grill and the number one selling item on our lunch menu for all those 40 years.

When my partners Mike and Richard and I developed the concept for The Grill we wanted to differentiate it from the national steak houses. In addition to having the finest Prime steaks, chops, and fresh seafood, we wanted to have some comfort food. The obvious choice was Chicken Pot Pie. Today, steaks at The Grill on the Alley are in the $65 range while the Chicken Pot Pie is $27.75. Conventional wisdom in the restaurant community was not to offer something for less money than the rest of the entrees. Even though The Grill was predominately a steak restaurant, there was bound to be one person who wanted another option and we would provide it. I believe if you give people what they want they will come back time and time again. One time they may order the Chicken Pot Pie, another time steak or fresh seafood. The Chicken Pot Pie became the number two best-selling item on the lunch menu behind the Cobb Salad and it was so successful that we added it to the dinner menu. Our guests were people who went out to fancy restaurants all the time. Chicken Pot Pie was something off the radar – unexpected.

With the success of our signature Chicken Pot Pie, we started adding other comfort foods to our menu, including Meat Loaf, which was unheard of for a high-end dinner house in Beverly Hills— and it all started in an apartment kitchen.

We were one of the first restaurants in the nation to elevate comfort food to fine dining and it did not go unnoticed.

A month after we opened, we got our first review in the now departed *Herald Examiner*. By the following month we had made it in the *Los Angeles Times*. In November of 1984, just 10 months after we opened, we had our first national review a glowing review in *Gourmet* magazine. It started with, "Imagine

L.L. Bean opening an outlet next door to Bijan or Giorgio and displaying its trademark Maine hunting shoes in the windows, and you have an idea of how a restaurant serving the likes of corned beef hash, and rice pudding fits in with the Beverly Hills chichi eating places." To John Sola's credit, it was all about the food. There wasn't a word about our notable Hollywood scene. In the final line of the *Gourmet* review it actually said, "Reservations are advisable during peak dining hours."

In 1986, the Los Angeles Times wrote of The Grill's weekly short rib special: "Short ribs are not the kind of food you would expect to find at a fine dining restaurant." Yet with the influence of The Grill, short ribs became a staple on chefs' menus across the country from The French Laundry to Roy Choi's Kogi truck.

We liked that our traditional grill was different from any

other dinner house in Los Angeles. None of this could have been done without Chef John Sola. He was the most important hire of my career. He possessed a meticulous ability to follow recipes and he trained his staff to do the same. John was an excellent cook and willing to cook our straight-forward cuisine without trying to make it fancy. His single-minded obsession has always been consistency, which is one of the main reasons The Grill thrived in the world's most fickle city. He and I both always believed that the best compliment we could get – and we did – was that someone loved The Grill because it was so consistent: from the way we took reservation on the phone, to the way our guests were greeted at the front door, to the table service, to the drinks coming from the bar, and of course, to the dishes coming out of the kitchen. John's philosophy was that to be a great chef, you had to be a great teacher, and how good you were as a teacher showed in the consistency of the dishes coming from your kitchen.

In John's kitchen a medium-rare steak always has to be medium-rare. His recipes didn't call for chopped parsley but *finely* chopped parsley. He used only classic sauces like Bearnaise and Hollandaise, some of which took days to prepare. Herbs had to be hand-picked from their stems. Years later, when I ordered a dish and it came garnished with parsley—with stems attached—I knew John Sola didn't have anything to do with that restaurant.

Bob Spivak, seated, and Chef John Sola testing out new recipes at The Grill on the Alley, 1984

It reminded me of when I was 13 and working in my father's commissary. My job was to take a 100-pound sack of navy beans and sort through them to make sure there were no rocks left in the bag of beans. The beans we bought were all sorted by machine and if a rock was the same size as a bean, the sorter would miss it. My dad always stressed the fact that it took only one rock to ruin someone's meal, and possibly cause a broken tooth. I didn't think about the 99 people who didn't get a rock in their barbecue beans; I worried about the one who did. Now, parsley stems won't break a tooth, but when John placed parsley on a plate, you never saw the stems. That was the level of detail John taught all his cooks.

John absolutely insisted that the people working in the kitchen did not know who was sitting at which table. He didn't care if it was Johnny Carson or John Nee from Carson, he had the same exacting standards for every dish that left his kitchen.

Not only did every dish need to taste consistent, but every plate needed to look consistent. John tried to give our dishes a signature "Grill" look: traditional without being overly precious or contrived. Holding a plate, he used to tell his cooks who were used to a more continental style of presentation, "This is how you used to do it," then he would shake the plate so everything was a little less precise and little bit roughed up and say, "Now this is The Grill."

Plates would be placed on the table in exactly the same way, every time: protein in the front and if it is steak or a piece of meat, the fat must be facing away from the diner. John was from the school of traditional chefs who believe that food should be arranged on the plate from right to left because that is the direction most people eat, no matter whether they are left- or right-handed. Vegetables, starches and condiments all also had their set positions on the plate. Although it was a running joke in the kitchen between the cooks and the servers, the net effect was that it made every plate coming out of our kitchen look consistent, and that was the goal. Those dishes that are still on the menu 40 years later and still look exactly the same.

The soups were all hearty, none overly pureed, and the house soups were the tomato broth-based Manhattan Clam Chowder (because everyone did white chowder), and a thick and hearty Gazpacho that originally came from Scandia. The Grill also wouldn't be The Grill without its signature bread. We knew that to be *legit* we had to have the perfect crusty sourdough bread, just like the traditional San Francisco grills.

While we were trying to channel the past, we also wanted to make our dishes current and standouts. At the time, most salads in other restaurants – like Cobb and Niçoise – were served in rows, so you might have a row of chicken next to a row of bacon next to a row of avocado for a Cobb salad. John tossed all of our salads in the kitchen so that every fork-full could be a mixture of the flavors. It seems funny to think about now, but the idea of tossing salads was an innovation for the time. The Grill's

Cobb, our most popular dish, was also diced slightly larger than the Brown Derby's version. I've always said while the Brown Derby invented the Cobb, we made it famous.

Chapter 9
Opening Jitters

In November 1983 we were just about finished with the construction of The Grill when someone from the Beverly Hills building department came to inspect the premises and asked, "Where are the fire sprinklers?"

"We don't have fire sprinklers," I answered. When he told me they were required, I said, "We have an approved set of plans stamped by the Beverly Hills building department, and they don't call for fire sprinklers."

The inspector said, "I don't care what the building department said or did, I'm in charge of the construction and if I say I'm requiring the building to have sprinklers, the building will have sprinklers."

I went back to the building department and they told me that if the building inspector required sprinklers, we had to put them in. But, in order to install fire sprinklers, you must dig up the street to connect to the main sewer line. It was November, the beginning of the holiday season. When I went to get the permit for work, I was told we were not allowed to dig up the street during the holiday season. Therefore, we had to wait until January 2 to start the project. We used the delay to hire the staff.

John Sola recruited several of the team members from his former restaurant to come over to The Grill which provided a nucleus of dining room and kitchen workers. I had hired a bookkeeper and assistant named Donna Sloate. Donna did everything from scheduling all my appointments to setting up our bookkeeping systems. When it came time to advertise for restaurant help, Donna ran an ad in the *Los Angeles Times* which read:

NEW EXCLUSIVE RESTAURANT OPENING IN BEVERLY HILLS

looking for all restaurant positions.

Everybody interested come to 9560 Dayton Way between the hours of 9 to 5.

Only professionals need apply.

The next morning, Donna was downstairs in the restaurant and I was upstairs in the office/storeroom when the first job seeker arrived. Donna hurried upstairs to tell me the first server applicant was *perfect* for the position, and I should come down and interview him right away. His name was Hector Camacho and he *was* perfect. Hector had a lot of serving experience, was tall, handsome, and had an engaging personality. I hired him on the spot. (It is now 40 years later and Hector is still with The Grill as the evening maître d' and has become part of our family.)

The rest of the day, Donna interviewed potential employees and determined who would get a second interview with me. (Donna would stay on as the bookkeeper and assistant to the managing partner for the next 10 years.)

John brought Israel Camacho over from the Chronicle to work the broiler, and like Hector, Israel is still with The Grill and now is the Head Chef. In his first position as Broiler Chef, Israel was responsible for all the meats that were cooked over the oak charcoal. Before each night, Issy, as he was called, would let me know he intended to "pitch a shutout." Shutout was a baseball metaphor that, in this case, meant that there would be no steaks coming back to the kitchen because they were not cooked to the exact order. (Despite having the same last name, Hector and Israel are not related.)

On Monday, January 30, 1984, almost two years since the lunch meeting at the Bel-Air Sands Hotel where Mike, Richard, and I became partners and Leslie reentered my life, I went to The Grill on the Alley to finish preparing for Tuesday's opening...an opening that might not happen given what I found. One of the chandeliers lay broken on the floor!

Each chandelier had eight arms and each arm held a glass globe. The chandelier didn't have a safety chain to keep it anchored in one place and when the night cleaning crew came in, they had spun the chandelier around to clean each of the globes, thereby loosening the entire works. With the help of my partners, we were able to get a team in that afternoon to repair the chandelier and even traced down nine replacement antique glass globes just before midnight, one for each of the eight arms and one large globe for the center of the chandelier.

That crisis averted, I made sure everyone scheduled to work would be there. I looked over the restrooms to make sure they were clean and fully stocked and double-checked that the air conditioning and heat were operational. I checked the reservation sheets (there were no reservations), and made sure the night cleaning crew was all set to do a final cleaning. Then I went home.

The morning of January 31 promised sun and comfortable temperatures in the 70s; another beautiful day in Beverly Hills. When I arrived at 8 a.m., another unwelcome surprise awaited. One of the eight-inch glass chandelier globes on the chandelier that had been replaced the day before had come loose during the night and crashed into pieces on a chair; a chair someone would have been sitting on at table 11 if we had been open. I immediately got a ladder to check and tighten the remaining seven glass globes myself; they were all fine, but we were minus one glass globe for the opening.

Chef John Sola and I went over the menus and checked that we had all the necessary ingredients, an unnecessary exercise as it turns out John was the most organized of all of us and had everything under control.

At precisely 11 a.m. I walked across the black and white checked marble floor, past the white-linen covered tables and green leather booths, took a deep breath, and unlocked the mahogany-framed glass doors. In a moment of panic, I worried that maybe the alley location had been a terrible idea and no one would be able to find us, so I carried a bar chair out to the sidewalk and propped a Now Open sign, that Donna printed on her computer, on the seat. *This was it.* All the months of planning, building, hiring, ordering, arranging, and agonizing were over. *The Grill on the Alley was open.*

Opening day crew at The Grill on the Alley, January 31, 1984

Chapter 10
The Grill on The Alley

Our first customer, or guest, as we preferred to call them, walked in at 11:30 a.m. It was a single man who worked for Van Cleef & Arpels, a luxury jewelry store just down the street on Rodeo Drive. He ordered a bottle of Crystal Champagne ($100), Caesar Salad, New York Steak, and Cheesecake for dessert. His bill was over $150, which in 1984 was a lot of money. We were excited to think the lunch checks could average over $100 per person! But when I asked him if he ate like that every day, he said he had just sold a diamond ring for $150,000 and was celebrating. In the 40-year history of The Grill, no single person has ever spent that much money for lunch.

That first day, we served about 25 lunches, or covers as they are known in the industry, and about the same number for dinner. The second day was about the same. Then things started to pick up. By the beginning of the second week, we served around 100 lunches and 75 dinners. By the third week, we were turning people away who didn't have lunch reservations.

Most of the lunch reservation requests were for 1 p.m. In order to get two seatings from every table, we couldn't take a lot of 1 p.m. reservations because you couldn't seat the tables at noon and expect to have them available for a 1 p.m. seating. And, you couldn't expect to have people coming in for lunch at 2:30 p.m. I started asking the people who wanted the 1 p.m. time slot where they were coming from and found the majority were agents from one of the talent agencies in the neighborhood. When I realized the entertainment industry generally lunched at 1 p.m., I devised a plan.

We had 32 tables and I needed to have those tables occupied

by noon or 12:30 so they would be free between 1 and 1:30 p.m. for a second turn. I set up the reservation sheet to take 20 reservations at noon and 12 reservations at 12:30 p.m. Then at 1 p.m. I would only take three reservations. If someone wanted a 1 p.m. reservation I would tell them 1:15 or 1:30 was all that was available. There was so much demand for reservations that my plan worked great. When someone called, and the time slot was taken, we could move them earlier or later. The regular customers all came to know me and would ask for me by name. I could then talk to them and adjust the reservation time, depending on how regular a guest they were.

When "walk-ins" came in at noon I would let them know I could seat them, but they had to be out by 1 p.m. They thought I was crazy because at noon the dining room was empty. I assured them that by 1 p.m. the restaurant would be teeming with people and all the tables would be full. If the guest was hesitant, I would give them my business card and ask them to call me personally when they wanted a reservation. That way they knew I was being honest and that I valued their business. Those who agreed to give us the table back by 1 p.m. would stay. Rarely did anyone fail to give us the table back by the agreed upon time.

Thirteen of our tables were booths. The Grill's booths are one of the few status symbols in Hollywood that can't be bought and the Hollywood Reporter dubbed them as "moguls-only booths." The power players each had their favorites depending on whether they wanted privacy, publicity, or people watching. As I had learned from hosting at the Redwood, everyone wanted a booth.

By this time, I was familiar with the regulars and their seating preferences. I knew which guests needed a booth and which ones would be amenable to a table seating if all the booths were reserved. This became difficult when people would see empty booths and request booth seating. Empty didn't always mean available; it meant the booth was open for those guests who had requested a booth at the time they made their reservation. When I had one or two booths empty, I would set a bottle of wine on the table. That way, when I seated someone at a nearby table, they would assume the booth was occupied.

One night a regular came in insisting that he absolutely had to have a booth because he was meeting a group of investors who had flown in from out-of-town. We didn't have one available – he was furious – but when we sat his party at a table across from Madonna and Sean Penn's table (they weren't at a booth either), we made their night.

I quickly discovered there was a hierarchy amongst the talent agents and once I got to know the higher-ranking agents, I was able to seat them at the coveted booths. The William Morris Agency was very important to our success, and I paid special attention to them, blocking out more 1:15 p.m. and 1:30 p.m. time slots to make sure I could take care of all their agents who regularly brought clients to The Grill. Before I knew it, just about every big Hollywood Star was coming in for lunch. When big celebrities are seen eating at a restaurant, the other guests tell their friends, and their friends tell other friends. In 1984, word-of-mouth was better than Twitter, Facebook, TikTok, or any other form of social media which had yet to be created.

Now, I wasn't exactly cut out to deal with celebrities. Growing up, all I was interested in was baseball and girls. I never went to the movies and didn't know one star from another. I'm the guy who called Robert Mitchum "Mr. Douglas" when he walked through the door, thinking he was Kirk Douglas. But I learned and made sure the high-visibility celebrities had a quiet booth away from the crowd so they could relax with their guests and not be bothered for autographs.

One day Ron Meyer came in for lunch. Ron was one of the founding partners of Creative Artists Agency, which was one of the two largest and most successful talent agencies in the world. I didn't have his name down on my reservation list that day. My father had taught me to *never tell the guest he wasn't on the list* because it may have been our mistake, or his assistant had forgotten to call. I just said, "right this way" and seated him in a small table for two in the center of the room. A few minutes later, in walked Jane Fonda, asking for Ron Meyer. I had a reservation under her name, but didn't know she was with Ron. She sat down at that small table and they had lunch together. The next time Ron came in I apologized to him about seating him at such a small table. "Anytime you are having lunch with a big star, I'll always have a quiet booth for you." He thanked me and I seated him at the same little table. Ten minutes later, in walked Candice Bergen. She sat down at that small table with Ron, just as Jane Fonda had done before. Ron never said a thing—that's the kind of person he is.

By the third week, dinner was as busy as lunch. Never in my entire restaurant career did I have more demand for reservations than we had tables. Everyone wanted 7 p.m. and 7:30 p.m. reservations. We started pushing the people who were not regulars to 6:30 p.m. and 8:30 p.m. When those slots were full, we said the 6 and 9 p.m. openings were the best reservations we had.

One Tuesday night about four weeks after opening, I received so many calls that I couldn't say NO to. I just kept saying yes, and of course, I was terribly over-booked. I was in so much trouble I had to wait for the 6 p.m. people to get up before I could seat the 7 p.m. reservations and, as the night went on, the situation only worsened. Everyone was yelling at me, wanting to know why they couldn't be seated. One special guest, Clare Winer, approached me and said, "I see you are having a lot of trouble seating people. Would you like us to go somewhere else tonight?"

"If you're serious," I said, "tell me where you would like to go and I'll make a reservation for you."

She wanted to go to Trader Vic's. I called the restaurant, explained the problem, and they gave her a table. I told her the next time they came in dinner was on me. She and her husband Steve became regular weekly customers. I never forgot her kindness on that night.

The 1980s were a different time for restaurants. Think "Dallas," "Dynasty," and Gordon Gekko: it was an era defined by big hair, big shoulder pads and hostile takeovers. Cocktails at lunch were commonplace, as were extravagant bottles of wine at both lunch and dinner, and Dom Perignon was a big seller. Cigarette smoking wasn't banned in Beverly Hills until 1987. Drexell Burnham Lambert's Beverly Hills office was across the street – this was Michael Milken's firm that invented the junk bond – and our regular customers included Drexell bankers. It was a time of big spending and celebrated excess on all fronts.

We did everything possible to accommodate our guests. We opened house accounts for them. All someone had to do was give me a business card and sign their check. If someone had an account and they brought in a friend, I would open an account for their friend as well. This whole process of opening a house account with just a business card made people feel special. I felt they would make sure they paid their Grill account first because they needed to keep coming in with clients and guests.

We had a list of agents who were approved "to sign," and if an agent wanted to sign who wasn't on the list – this was in the days before cell phones – we would tell them they had a phone call at the maître d' stand. When they came up to the front, we would discretely tell them the bad news —they weren't on the approved list—and that in order to sign their check they would have to get their agency's Controller on the phone to give us the go ahead. A junior agent would sooner grovel to their Controller than let on to a client that he or she wasn't on the list at The Grill; there was a lot of calling of Controllers in those days. We continued this policy for several years and it was a rare occurrence that we had to close an account due to an unpaid bill.

In my previous restaurant experiences, answering the phones was never a problem. At The Grill, it was a big problem, but in a good way. We had four lines coming into our rotary telephone and every afternoon, all four lines would be lit up with people wanting to make reservations. One afternoon I was overwhelmed. I needed a 30-minute break from the phones to organize the reservations and decided to take all four lines off the hook. That way, everyone who called got a busy signal. After a half hour of peace and quiet I put one line back into service. This worked pretty well until the phone company called. It seems that in the 30 minutes I had the phones off the hook, the phone company received over 25 calls reporting that our phones were out of order! They warned me if I did this again, they would charge us. From that time on, I hired someone just to deal with the phone. It turned out that was not enough, and we needed a second person.

I set up the reservation list for 12 reservations at 6 and 9 p.m., and each half-hour thereafter. That way, whoever answered the phones could only take a reservation if there was an open line on the reservation sheet. If there wasn't an open line, the person was trained to say, "I'm sorry, that time is taken. The closest time I have would be..." and they'd provide the caller with the timeslot corresponding to the next open line on the sheet. If someone wanted a time which was full, and they knew enough to ask for Bob, I would talk to them and figure something out. I learned fast that I needed to block out some times at 7, 7:30, 8, and 8:30 p.m. so when people asked for me, I could take their reservation without overbooking.

One day I took a call from a rather exasperated sounding woman. She said she was getting 15 or 20 calls a *day* from people dialing the wrong number. It seems her phone number was one number off from The Grill's telephone number. She told me *we* were going to have to change our phone number. I told her we couldn't do that but to please come in with a friend and I would buy them dinner. She turned my offer down and said, "I'll fix you" and hung up the phone.

The following Saturday night at 8 p.m., the busiest night and time of the week, I had 10 different parties come in claiming they had reservations – reservations which I didn't have. Then I figured it out. The lady who was getting the "wrong number" calls was pretending to take their reservations. Well, I was done playing nice. I called her and said if she didn't stop taking reservations, I would have my lawyer contact her. This must have scared her because the mysterious reservations stopped and I never heard from her again.

After we were open about six weeks, I realized we needed to hire a second host to seat people. I ran an ad and a young man named Jeffrey Best applied for the job. I could tell from the first day he was going to catch on fast. I was excited to have someone as sharp as Jeff who understood the clientele and what we were trying to do to make all our guests comfortable.

The second day Jeffrey was scheduled to work, he didn't show up. "No call no show" is about the worst thing you can do when working in a restaurant. The next morning, he called me. I was sure he had worked his last day at The Grill on the Alley— until he told me his story.

Jeffrey had a very fancy MG sports car that was not registered. Now that he was working, he wanted to drive the car. He took the license plates off his Volkswagen and put them on the MG. While he was driving to the restaurant, he was pulled over by a Beverly Hills policeman. When the officer discovered the license plates were not registered to the car Jeff was driving, they arrested him. The next day, he got out of jail and came directly to work.

This story touched my heart. "Everyone deserves a second chance," I told him. And, while I believe this, I also told him there were no third chances. Well, l made the correct decision because he became one of the most valuable team members we had and was with us for five years. Jeffrey also knew who the celebrities were and made sure I knew "who was who." (Later, when we opened Daily Grill, Jeffrey became co-manager of The Grill, along with Allan Ludwig.)

Jason Spivak and Jeffrey Best at The Grill on The
Alley, late 1980s

One night while Jeffrey was working, a man came in on a date and demanded a booth. Jeffrey told him that all of the booths were reserved and seated the couple at a table. When the server came over to get their drink order, the man ordered a bottle of Dom Perignon. All of our Dom and finest wines were kept in a locked liquor cabinet in the locked office upstairs and a manager had to sign-out each bottle so we could track the inventory. So, Jeffrey went upstairs, unlocked the office, unlocked the liquor cabinet, got the bottle, logged the bottle, locked the liquor cabinet, locked the office and went back downstairs. The server presented the bottle to the guest and when the man tasted the champagne he said, "It's turned, I want a new bottle."

Jeffrey, who was still new at the time, went back upstairs and did the entire routine again – unlocked the office, unlocked the liquor cabinet, logged the champagne, locked the cabinet, locked the office – and brought down a second bottle of Dom. The server presented the second bottle, opened it, and when the man tasted it, he said again, "It's turned. I want another bottle."

Jeffrey took the bottle behind the bar, and when the man wasn't looking, he and the bartender tasted the champagne. There was nothing wrong with the Dom; the man was just angry that he didn't get a booth. I remember Jeffrey called me at home to ask me how to handle the situation, and I told him, "Just tell the guy we're out of Dom." Jeffrey told him, the couple ordered two glasses of wine and ate their dinner: problem solved.

During that time, Jeffrey became friends with Ken Jones, a young financier working for a company in the neighborhood. Years later they became partners and formed Best Events, a company specializing in planning large events such as the Sundance Film Festival. In just a few short years they had the largest event planning company on the West Coast. Several years later they opened their first restaurant, Habana, in Costa Mesa. Now, they own several restaurants and bars in the Los Angeles area. Whenever Jeffrey introduces me to someone, he always tells them I am his mentor. That makes me feel very special and proud.

By this time the only meal period that wasn't sold out was Saturday lunches. I was working Monday through Friday from 9 a.m. to 10 p.m. and Saturdays from 4 p.m. to 10 p.m. I took Saturday lunch off. One Saturday during lunch, a "big shot agent" came in from William Morris. He told Norman Church, our Saturday maître d', that he had heard a lot about the restaurant from people in his office and wanted to come in that night with four people at 7:30 p.m. Norman told him we were totally booked up and would not be able to accommodate him on such short notice. Well, this agent was very unhappy and stormed out of the restaurant. He returned one hour later with his scrapbook to show Norman all the important people he represented, including many big actors and the President of the United States. Norman called me, told me the story, and I told Norman to take him. By this time, I had two reservations blocked out at each half-hour for people who were regulars and called late and I gave this agent one of my spots. From that time on, the agent became a regular.

Several years later, the head of a rival agency once gave me a hard time because he thought that I was seating William Morris agents first, and I said to him, "You've been coming here for a while, but William Morris has been here since day one. William Morris took me to this dance, and I plan to go home with them." The rival agency boycotted for a week or two, but then came back.

Then there was the time Allan Ludwig, our maître d', took a call in the middle of a very busy night for a reservation in the next ten minutes for a Mr. Eastwood. When Clint Eastwood came through the door, Allan didn't have a table for him. Allan told me, "He said his name was Mr. Eastwood. He didn't say Clint Eastwood."

Besides being The Grill's maître d', Allan was also an investor. He had extensive customer service experience—he had owned a men's clothing store but had never worked in a restaurant. Also, having grown up on the West Side of Los Angeles, he knew a lot of people, so I agreed to teach him how to work the door at night. It took me about six months to teach Allan the front of the house. He learned fast "under fire" and became very popular with our guests.

The tricky thing was you had to be able to get the regulars and celebrities, who absolutely refused to wait, to their tables without letting the people who were waiting know that someone was getting seated ahead of them. My father had taught me all kinds of tricks of the trade that he had used at the Redwood that I in turn taught to Allan. For example: if someone comes in at 8 p.m. and we tell them we are running 20 minutes behind, and then one of our impatient regulars comes in after, we would say, "Hello, Mr. Jones, your party is already here. Let me show you to your table," even if they were the first ones in their party to arrive. The host would take them to the table while the maître d' would continue to massage those waiting guests.

I honestly believe that maître d' at The Grill is probably one of the most challenging and stressful jobs anywhere, ever. It is an art, not a science, and being able to think on your feet is essential. Jeffrey once compared managing the front of the house at The Grill to "throwing the pieces of a jigsaw puzzle up in the air and trying to put the puzzle together before any of the pieces hit the ground." That about sums it up.

Initially, we had hired an old-school, professional maître d' named Roberto, who looked like he had been sent by central casting. He was impeccably dressed and perfectly put together like Ralph Fiennes' character in the movie "The Grand Budapest Hotel," but by the following Monday after we opened, when the phones started ringing nonstop, Roberto started to crack. He may have looked the part but he couldn't play the part...at least not at The Grill.

By the end of the second week, when our bar area was standing-room only, it was clear he was in over his head. I remember Roberto saying to me one night as he was leaving, "The way you're running this place, you'll never do 200 dinners." He walked out our mahogany door on the alley that night and never walked through it again: no phone call, no "I quit," he just vanished. By the next week, we were doing 200 dinners every night of the week, sometimes even 300, in a restaurant with 120 seats.

Beyond the who's who and massaging the egos, what is so difficult about running the front of the house is that to do it right, you really do have to book heavily enough to make sure all the tables are full all the time, otherwise, you are leaving money on the table. Which means that on any given night, reservations can easily run 10 or 15 minutes behind.

I used to test people; I had to know who was willing to wait five minutes at lunch and who had to be seated immediately. Even when a person's table was ready, I might say, "John, just give me a couple of minutes," to see how they reacted. If they lost it, then I knew never again, but if they were willing to go to the bar and have an iced tea, or chat with me about sports, then I knew on the days when we inevitably got backed up, that these were the people who would be willing to wait 5 or 10 or 15 minutes. I spent much of my afternoon and night talking to guests to keep their minds off the wait. Some days we would get so backed up I would have to make conversation for 20 or 30 minutes and by the time their table finally came up, I had a new best friend.

On another Saturday night, the restaurant was full and I was about a half-hour behind on seating people. A woman came in and gave me her name and I checked the reservation sheet. Her name wasn't on it. When this happened, I would ask a series of questions to find the reservation, determine if it was our mistake, or discover if she was trying to get into the restaurant without a reservation. Sometimes another person in the party would make the reservation and I would find it by giving the names of the people on my list. When that didn't work, I would ask how long ago she made the reservation; you had to call at least a week ahead to get an 8 p.m. reservation on a Saturday night.

She said she made the reservation two weeks ago. I asked if she talked to a man or a woman; she said it was a woman, which would be correct, and I assumed it was our mistake. I told her to please bring her party into the bar and I would buy all of them a drink and seat them soon. She went outside.

Now, I don't know what made me do this, but I followed her out and heard her tell her friends she got a table. Her friend said, "I don't know who you know to get us into The Grill without a reservation at 8 o'clock on a Saturday night, but it must be someone very important."

Aha! She never did have a reservation. When she came back into the restaurant, I called her over, so as not to embarrass her in front of her friends. I explained I had heard her friend's surprise that she was able to get a table without a reservation. I then told her my offer to buy them a drink still stood; however, it would take me one hour to get her a table. They waited for the table, had a good time, and she thanked me on her way out with a wink in her eye. I dodged a bullet and made a happy guest.

I was quite satisfied with the way that situation came out. If I hadn't overheard the conversation, I would have seated her party ahead of other people who had already been waiting, which wouldn't have been fair. Also, I made a friend out of a situation that could have been ugly.

When situations like this arise, it's important to remember that even though she wasn't telling the truth, all she wanted to do was to come in and spend her money with us. I don't know if she ever came back but my guess would be that she did.

***

One night at 8 p.m. the restaurant was crazy busy. A very tall man, standing at least 6'4" and wearing a full-length mink coat, approached and put his arm around me. "Do you know who I'm here with?" he asked. He then proceeded to tell me he was with Ed Hookstratten (known as "The Hook") and told me it would be a good idea if I got them seated. I didn't know who Ed Hookstratten was, but the name sounded familiar; I figured I'd better get them a table.

I alerted Allan that I needed the next available table for two. When the table came up, I seated Mr. Hookstratten and his guest at table 10. This was the most difficult of the 32 tables to seat as it was a small deuce (two-places) right next to the bus station where the dishes are stacked after the servers clear the tables. The two men sat down and had dinner. Later, Leslie and I sat at booth 3 and were having our dinner. Mr. Hookstratten walked toward me and I stood up to thank him.

He told me he liked the restaurant very much and wanted to have a standing reservation for lunch every day at 1 p.m. Further, he wanted to sit in booth 3 where Leslie and I were seated. Now, I couldn't swear to this, but I think the reason he picked booth number 3 was that it was the third booth back from the door: far enough away to not be bothered by the people sitting at the bar yet it could be seen by most people walking by who all wanted to see who Hook was sitting with. I also thought that maybe seeing Leslie and me at the booth, he thought if we were sitting there, it must be a good table. The fact was, we sat anywhere there was an open table!

My naivete showed when I said, "Well, Mr. Hookstratten, I don't take standing reservations because they never work out. Sometimes you may not be able to make it for lunch and then I'm stuck holding the table for the entire meal period. Also, I would not be able to guarantee you a specific booth at 1 p.m. because I need to use the tables twice each lunch period." I further explained that if he wanted to reserve a specific table, he would have to be seated no later than 12:30 p.m.

"Let me get this straight," he said. "If I want to come in every day, I have to have my assistant call for a reservation—every day—and if I want table number 3, I have to come in at 12:30. Is that correct?"

If I had known then exactly who this man was, I would have taken Hook's standing reservation at 1 p.m.! It turns out Hook was a very powerful, well-known lawyer and agent for news broadcasters, television personalities, and sports figures and he brought one of his clients in for lunch every day. His clients included people like Johnny Carson, national evening news anchor Dan Rather, sportscaster Vin Scully, Los Angeles Raiders football star Marcus Allan, late night talk show host Tom Snyder, KABC news anchor Cynthia Allison, news anchor Paul Moyer, and many others I came to know over the years.

People would come into the restaurant just to see who was sitting with him. For the next 30 years, Hook's assistant made a 12:30 p.m. reservation every single day, and Hook ordered the Chicken Pot Pie at least once a week. He became one of the three most important guests The Grill ever had.

About two weeks after my conversation with Hook, Allan answered the phone one evening; the caller asked for me. It was Johnny Carson. Johnny was calling from his car phone, which I didn't even know existed in 1984. He wanted to come in for dinner. It was 7:30 on a Friday night.

"Johnny, when do you want to come in?" I asked. "Now," he answered. "I'll be there in 10 minutes."

"Well, it's going to take about an hour before I can seat you," I told him. "And it may not be a booth."

Johnny drove around for an hour and came in with his wife, Alex. I seated them at a small table on the side of the restaurant. He became a wonderfully loyal customer, always on the quiet side, who loved our mashed potatoes and liked to drink Jordan wine. In some way, I felt he respected me for not just taking him on the spot. For years later, every time he saw me, he would tell whoever he was with that I was the young man who made him wait an hour for a table, and laugh. He came to The Grill with The Hook a lot and always kidded me about that night.

There was another night early-on when we had to put Sylvester Stallone at our noisiest, smallest table by the busser's station, and Stallone ate his dinner – shrimp cocktail, ground beef and tomatoes – without a complaint. During another ridiculously busy lunch in those first weeks, Dustin Hoffman was waiting in the bar and called Allan over and said, "I don't have a reservation, but do you think there might be a table available soon?" Twenty minutes later, this same table became available and Allan warned him that it was a tough, small table next to the busser's station. Dustin Hoffman said it was no problem, and ate lunch. On the way out, he stopped to thank Allan and added, "And you're right; it is a terrible table." Dustin Hoffman became a regular too.

Jerry Breslauer, one of the three people who I consider as the most important guests of The Grill, would come in for lunch and dinner with his clients at least four times a week. Jerry was a Business Manager for many high-visibility clients including director Steven Spielberg, Walt Disney Studios Chairman Jeffrey Katzenberg, Bruce Springsteen, Michael Jackson, and musical producer and film studio executive David Geffen. Jerry was a weekday regular for more than 30 years and was the first person to ever bring The Boss (Bruce Springsteen) to The Grill.

Every Saturday, Jerry would bring in his 80+ year old mother, Tilly. It was a ritual. He would take Tilly to get her hair done and then come into The Grill for lunch. She was such a nice, stately woman who all the team members at The Grill just loved her. When they came in, the entire wait staff would come to her table to say hello. This was very rewarding for me because that was what The Grill was all about; making people feel at home.

The third significant guest on my list was Dick Carroll. Dick owned the very popular men's clothing store, Carroll & Co., the haberdashery of Beverly Hills which was just down the street from The Grill. Dick, who had been an old-time Warner Bros. publicist, opened his store in the 1950s and dressed movie stars like Fred Astaire, Gene Kelly, Carry Grant, and Kirk Douglas. I still remember when he had lunch with Fred Astaire; the entire restaurant was abuzz.

Dick had once owned a restaurant named The Saloon, which was open several years before The Grill but closed before we opened. One day Dick called me aside and said he thought "The Grill was a brilliant restaurant and the front door in the alley was genius." He went on to say, "If my restaurant was like yours, we would still be open and very successful." I considered that one of the greatest compliments I ever received.

The Grill on The Alley – Beverly Hills, CA

Ed Hookstratten, Jerry Breslauer, and Dick Carroll raised the popularity of The Grill with their continued patronage. The perception was that if any of those three men were regulars at The Grill, it was the place to be.

***

Every Sunday night we served Prime Rib. Each Sunday, the wife of a high-visibility celebrity would come in and place five orders of Medium Rare Prime Rib; three orders for herself and two friends to eat at the restaurant, and two orders to take home for her dogs.

One Sunday night the Chef came to me and said he was going to be sold out of Prime Rib before this special lady came in; he didn't know what to do. It was too late to cook another Rib order, so we called the nearby Lawry's Prime Rib. We were very good friends with the management of Lawry's, and we traded Prime Ribs with them: one uncooked for one cooked. We brought the cooked rib back to the restaurant and when the woman ordered her usual five orders, we served the Lawry's Prime Rib to her. That same night we overheard her tell her friends "How much better The Grill's Prime Rib was than Lawry's." She had no idea she was actually eating the Lawry's Prime Rib.

***

While our focus has always been *quality without compromise,* we have never been too proud to modify our dishes to our customers' tastes. The "no modifications" trend was big in the '80s and made a big comeback among today's chefs, but at The Grill we had been telling guests "Yes" for more than three decades. In the 1980s, Loretta Swit from M.A.S.H. used to bring in her own whole wheat pasta for us to cook and order a plate of broccoli, steamed for 20 minutes. Yes, broccoli steamed for 20 minutes turns to mush, but no one ever said a word.

The first time that Woody Allen came in, he was with Diane Keaton. When our server Pablo went to take their order, Woody Allen told Pablo that what he really felt like was an omelet and could we make him an omelet even though it wasn't on the menu. Pablo said of course, what would he like? Woody Allen said that what he really felt like was an omelet with lox, and did we have lox? Pablo told him we didn't have lox but we had something even better: our homemade gravlax, which is a cured salmon. So, Woody Allen was served the first-ever Grill gravlax omelet. When Pablo brought it to their table, Diane Keaton leaned over and whispered to Woody Allen, "See! I told you they will make you whatever you want here!" They couldn't believe it.

***

Unfortunately, you can't please everyone. One night as a guest was leaving, he stopped to tell me how much he enjoyed the restaurant. He told me how great the food was, he loved the menu choices, and the service was impeccable. About 15 minutes later, he came back in screaming: the valet lost his car and he would never come back to this "terrible restaurant."

Another time the valet gave the wrong rental car to a guest. The mistake was discovered when the valet brought the second guest a car and that person realized it was the wrong car. Well, it seems they both had rented white Chevrolet Impalas, one from Budget Rent A Car and the other from Hertz. We called Hertz to find the contact information for the person who had rented the car that we mistakenly gave to another guest. Then we drove the second guest to his hotel and then to where the first car was located and exchanged the cars. These efforts put us on the winning end of this one. Both guests realized how hard we worked to smooth out the situation and both wrote a nice letter to me letting me know how much they appreciated the way we handled our mistake.

Then there was the time Neil Diamond pulled up in his Porsche at lunch. He left the car running at the curb, believing the valet would park it for him. After a one-and-a-half-hour lunch, he came out and his car was still running, right where he left it. He thought the valet was so good to anticipate his exit and park the car in the same spot. We didn't tell him there was no valet parking service during lunch.

***

February 1985 the restaurant was as busy as ever. I was still working 13-hour days from Monday through Saturday. Sundays I spent with my children. There was very little time for Leslie. We would spend the night together either at her house (I would leave at five in the morning before Todd and Dayna would wake up) or she would stay at my apartment and drive home at 5 a.m. She would come into the restaurant in the evening, sit at the bar with a bottle of Pellegrino and talk to people while she waited for me to be done so we could eat dinner together, usually around 10 p.m.

Diners at The Grill on the Alley, 1985

Every two weeks, our good friends Smokey and Judy would come in and sit with Leslie until around 10 p.m. when we would all sit down and have dinner. Smokey and Judy were very special to us. They were the first couple that were friends of both of us. On this particular night at dinner, we were talking about Lionel Richie's new album *"Can't Slow Down"* and decided to go to my apartment after dinner and listen to music.

Leslie and I drove together, and, on our way, she told me she was very upset. "You work six nights a week. The only time we get to see each other is at 10 p.m. for dinner. This is no life for me."

When we got to the apartment, I told her to go inside and I'd wait for our friends. When Smokey and Judy arrived, I explained this wasn't a good night to listen to music. They understood and drove away. When I went inside, Leslie stood with her hands on her hips and repeated, "This is no life for me! If you can't give me one night a week, alone, I'm going to have to move on."

I didn't have to think twice about that one! I said, "I won't work Tuesday nights ever again."

Allan Ludwig was off on Monday's and that is why I picked Tuesday. Leslie agreed that was a good solution. The next day when I woke up, I realized the first Tuesday of our agreement was Valentines Day — the second busiest night of the year behind New Years Eve. Well, there was no question in my mind. I would not be at The Grill for Valentine's night. Instead, I called Gigi, the manager of the Palm Restaurant, which was our big competition, and took Leslie there to celebrate Valentines Day—just the two of us. Everything at The Grill went great and I learned Allan and the team could run the restaurant for a night without me.

My partners and I hoped The Grill would do $3 million in sales that first year; the actual figure was over $5 million.

I'll never forget that day at the Bel-Air Sands Hotel — it was the beginning of The Grill on the Alley and my life with Leslie. The reality of it all was better than anything I could dream.

Chapter 11
Creating A Culture

The culture of teamwork and family we created at The Grill on the Alley was essential to our success. We never called the people who worked at the restaurant "employees," they were part of the team and therefore we called them "team members." I insisted they call me Bob and the chef, John.

In my opinion, as soon as you call someone Mr. or Miss, you put them on a different level. I didn't want that. If a table needed to be cleared, I didn't look for a busser, I cleared it myself. If there was a spill on the floor, I got the mop and cleaned it up. There wasn't anything we asked of them that we wouldn't do ourselves. My reasoning was they knew how hard John and I worked and that we had the attitude we were just part of the team. It wasn't necessary to set ourselves apart; they knew who was in charge.

My wife, Leslie, was very important to the culture. She had a great feel for the business and shared the values that governed how we treated guests and our team members. Leslie always had a smile on her face, was friendly with all the team members, and made the guests feel like family. She embraced The Grill as not just a business but as part of our social life as a couple.

We celebrated holidays and birthdays together and even had a softball team, which I also played on. We played other restaurant teams and some of the regular guests would put together a team and challenge us to a game. The Grill crew loved the fact I was right in there with them, and some were surprised that I was a good ball player.

We served a family meal twice a day before the lunch and dinner shifts. Everyone who worked at the restaurant could partake of this meal, and even though they might be working that night, we encouraged them to come in and share the family meal.

During the summer Leslie and I would invite the entire team to our house for a swimming party. In those days, we were closed on Sundays which allowed us to have all of them over.

When a guest was sick, we would call them and ask what night would be good for us to send dinner to their home and what would they like? When a team member was ill, we would call and see how they were feeling. If they were sick for a long period, Leslie and another team member and I would visit them. One time we had a manager in Chicago fall and had a serious injury while working. I flew to Chicago to visit her while she recuperated at home. Everyone in the restaurant knew about the visit; it demonstrated how much the entire company cared about its employees.

Some of The Grill team members were actors or entertainers. Whenever they performed locally, Leslie and I would attend their performance or concert. That's what family does and at The Grill we wanted everyone to feel like part of the family.

On the day before Thanksgiving, the chef would cook a traditional American Thanksgiving holiday dinner and we invited all the team members to bring their family, spouse, or a friend along. We wanted our team members to be proud of their restaurant and show it off to their friends. We also had many regular guests who would attend.

On Christmas we would have an "old fashioned" family Christmas party at the restaurant. Each team member received a gift (usually a clothing item with The Grill logo embroidered on it) and toys for their children. After the tragedy on September 11, 2001, our team voted to use the money we would spend for presents and send it to the relief fund for the Windows of the World which was the restaurant on top of the North Tower that was destroyed in the fire after terrorists flew an airplane into the building. Several of that restaurant's team members were killed in the blast. Our team was very proud of sending the money to their relief fund.

On January 31st of each year, we would celebrate the anniversary of the opening of The Grill. Oscar Zalaya was one of our long-time servers and his wife Gloria would make a special Tres Leche milk cake and decorate it commemorating the year of the anniversary. The chef would make a special team member meal that night – crab cakes or some other item from the menu. We'd reminisce about the history of The Grill and talk about the funny things that happened over the years.

One of the most important parts of being a good employer is communication. When someone went over and above what was required, we would recognize them at the team meeting which took place before every dinner shift. On the other hand, if someone was not performing up to standards, we would sit down with them, privately, and let them know what they needed to do to be successful at their job. If they repeated the same behavior, we would put in writing they had been verbally counseled and were still doing the same thing. If the behavior continued, they would lose their job. Clear communication about expectations and consequences are the responsibility of a good employer.

We didn't have to fire many team members as they respected us and realized this was the best restaurant job they would ever have. We treated them as we wanted to be treated. After growing up in this business and working in every restaurant job from washing dishes and cutting vegetables to acting as host, I could relate. If someone was scheduled to work but had something special to do that day, like a family event, we always made sure we could cover their shift and let them take the day off.

The results of our hard work were proven in later years by our stellar record for team member retention. After the restaurant was open for 20 years there were still 10 servers and 12 "Heart-of-the-House" team members who had started when we opened in 1984. Heart-of-the-House was our term for all the people working behind the scenes who aren't always seen by the guests like the cooks, dishwashers, prep cooks, and porters. Today, there are more than 10 team members still working at the restaurant who started when we opened in 1984.

As I've said before, everything I know about this business—good and bad—I learned from my father. But my mother also had a hand in laying the foundations of my future success. She dealt with my learning disabilities, problems in school, and failures throughout my 20s and 30s. She emphasized that all I needed to do was to be honest with her. I always knew I could count on her and as an adult, I could talk to her and never feel judged. She used to tell me that no matter how old your children were, you never stopped worrying about them. She taught me about ethics and the meaning of fair play, and thanks to her, I was never intentionally dishonest with a team member, guest, purveyor, or anyone else I negotiated with. "Honesty is the best policy" she would say, and I live by that principle.

Dad had a severe stroke in 1984, the year we opened. He couldn't walk, he couldn't talk, and he would get extremely frustrated. But when I pushed my wheelchair-bound father into The Grill on The Alley for the first time, while he couldn't communicate in any conventional way, I will never forget the look in his eyes—it was the look of a conquering hero.

Loving what you do every day is the greatest gift. My father loved what he did. I love what I do. He gave me that gift. None of it would have been possible without my father and mother. This is the culture we worked to create for our team members.

Chapter 12
Memorable Events from
"Hollywood's Clubhouse"

LA has always had its celebrity hangouts: The Brown Derby, Chasen's, Scandia, Le Dome, Ma Maison, Spago, Morton's, and somehow – by some confluence of factors that we had neither planned nor predicted – there we were, next in line in the lineage of Hollywood's greatest culinary landmarks, which made for many memorable events over the years.

Our guests in the 1980s included the legends Marlon Brando, Robert DeNiro, Dennis Hopper, Barbra Streisand, and Woody Allen. We also had the young stars of the moment like Molly Ringwald, Kevin Bacon, Robert Downey Jr., Johnny Depp, and brothers Charlie Sheen and Emilio Estevez. We had the couple of the decade, Sean Penn and Madonna, and then after they broke up Sean Penn continued to be a regular and Madonna would come in with Warren Beatty. We had comedians like Steve Martin, Chevy Chase, Martin Short, and Robin Williams. Michelle Pfeifer and her husband Peter Horton, who was an investor in the restaurant, were regulars. We had father and son, Kirk and Michael Douglas, both regulars.

The simple truth was that everybody who was anybody ate at The Grill. We had rock 'n roll icons like Bruce Springsteen and Sting. We had sports stars like Kareem Abdul Jabbar, Muhammad Ali, and Mike Schmidt. The list goes on and on: Dean Martin, Neill Simon, Harrison Ford, Jane Fonda, Bette Midler, Michael Caine, Barbara Walters, Tom Hanks, Rita Wilson, Olivia Newton-John, Tom Selleck, Christopher Plummer. If they were '80s superstars, they were eating at The Grill. We had become known as "Hollywood's Clubhouse."

Maybe it was the hidden alley entrance that made these celebrities feel as though they have escaped from the outside world, and they could be themselves. I also think the row of transom-like windows running along our 18-foot rear wall gave guests the sense of being underground and off the beaten path even in the heart of Beverly Hills. Bette Midler would come in, just off the set, with her hair in a towel. Anthony Hopkins, Kathleen Turner, and Ted Danson all routinely dined alone and would bring a book or an iPad, or just talk to our bartender. Actresses like Sofia Vergara and Drew Barrymore would come in wearing workout clothes and a baseball cap. For these guests, The Grill was like home.

The Grill was not the kind of place with autographed pictures on the walls, and despite the dozens of celebrities who walked through our doors each week, we almost never attracted paparazzi. When they did show up, like they did in packs with Katie Holmes, we discreetly escorted our guests out the back door while distracting the photographers at the entrance.

May I Introduce...

I think sometimes we assume that all famous people know each other, but it wasn't uncommon for a celebrity to get excited to spot another celebrity at The Grill, and sometimes to even ask our staff for an introduction. One day, Philadelphia Phillies third baseman and Hall of Famer, Mike Schmidt, was having lunch with agent Mike Ovitz at Ovitz's table 129. On the other side of the restaurant, Kevin Costner, a huge baseball fan, was eating lunch at table 106. Costner had just made "Field of Dreams" and just the year before had starred in "Bull Durham" in 1988.

Costner called Allan over to his table and asked if it was true that Mike Schmidt was in the restaurant. Schmidt was a legendary ball player – the best third baseman of all time – and was voted the best player in the Phillies' 100-year franchise history.

Kevin Costner asked Allan if he would mind introducing him to Schmidt. Allan's response to Costner was something like, "You want *me* to introduce *you*?" but then he went over to Schmidt and Ovitz's table, apologized for interrupting, and said there was a fan who would like to meet him: Kevin Costner. The admiration was mutual and when Mike Schmidt went over to Costner's table it was a half-hour love fest.

The Great One

One of our most legendary customers in the 1980s was Jackie Gleason. For my generation, there was no one greater than Gleason. A couple of years after we opened, he was in town shooting a movie and was staying at The Beverly Wilshire across the street from the restaurant. It was a five-minute walk but Jackie Gleason always arrived in a car with a driver. He ate dinner at The Grill every night he was in LA. We would have a double J&B Scotch waiting for him on the bar when he arrived, which he would finish by the time he made it to the other end of the bar. Setting his empty glass down on the far end of the bar, he would say to our bartender, "Another double, my man," which we would hand to him as he was walking to his table. He would usually have five or six by the time dessert arrived.

Unbeknownst to Jackie, our bartender and servers had a prearranged agreement with his wife, the dancer Marilyn Taylor (June Taylor's sister). While the first drink was a true double, the second one was quarter water, by the third drink it was half water and by the fifth drink it was water with a splash of Scotch. He always ordered steak and would take a bite of his steak, take a puff off his cigarette, and swig some Scotch, in that order. It turned out that during this period he was quietly battling cancer and he passed away the following year in 1987.

Always gregarious and larger than life, he truly was "The Great One."

You Only Compete Against Yourself

About a year after we opened The Grill on the Alley, I noticed a man standing in the dining room. He seemed more interested in looking at The Grill's kitchen than in being seated, I walked over to him and said, "You don't look like a customer. Are you in the restaurant business?"

The man met my gaze and in a very deep Southern drawl said, "Well no, I'm not in the restaurant business but I'm *going* in the restaurant business. I'm from Baton Rouge, Louisiana and I talked my favorite steakhouse into selling me a franchise. I'm opening it in Beverly Hills." The man's name was Paul Fleming.

Now, in 1985, opening a steakhouse was the last thing that sounded like a good idea given that food trends were going against red meat at the time. I thought, "Oh, you poor guy. This isn't time to open a steakhouse in Beverly Hills." (While The Grill had steaks on the menu, it wasn't the primary offering; therefore, The Grill wasn't considered a steakhouse.)

But what I said was, "Since you've never been in the restaurant business, if there's anything I can do to help you, I'd be happy to."

The name of his restaurant was Ruth's Chris. He needed a contractor, so I gave him our contractor's information. He also needed a public relations person, so I gave him Joan Luther's name; Joan was our PR person at The Grill.

As the months went by, this man would call me. I told him where to buy dishes and whatever else I could do to help this "poor man" get into the restaurant business.

Now, I didn't have to help him. He was actually going to compete with our business. His restaurant was only two blocks away from The Grill and the two main menu items were steak. But I always felt that the only competitor was yourself and if you do a great job with whatever the concept is, nobody else can touch you.

When Ruth's Chris opened, Paul invited me and Leslie to the opening. A year or two later he moved to Phoenix and called me. "Bob, you've got to come see what I'm doing!"

We flew to Phoenix and met Paul at his new restaurant – P.F. Chang's. The restaurants feature wok-cooked Asian cuisine prepared from scratch every day in every restaurant. Paul grew P.F. Chang's into one of the hottest restaurant companies in the country. He had a non-compete with Ruth's Chris that he couldn't open steakhouse for five years so when that expired, he opened Flemings, a national steakhouse.

I ran into Paul in Las Vegas sometime later and said, "Paul, I feel like the teacher whose student won the Nobel Prize."

Paul thanked me for the help I'd given him and told me how he had always appreciated the help to get started.

Totally Devoted

In June of 1986, the Van Cleef and Arpel store around the corner on Rodeo drive was taken over by an armed robber who held five people hostage. The story was all over the news. The standoff lasted more than 13 hours and all of downtown Beverly Hills was cordoned off with the streets filled with more than 80 police officers and S.W.A.T. Our main entrance was part of the area roped off by yellow police tape. A little before 1:00 we started hearing knocking on our back door on Wilshire Boulevard, which wasn't part of the cordoned off area. We thought it might be the police, but when we opened the door, it

119

was our regulars showing up for lunch that day.

You Can Fight City Hall

Beverly Hills was one small city surrounded by several different incorporated cities such as West Hollywood, Culver City, Santa Monica, and of course, Los Angeles. In 1986, just two years after we opened The Grill, the City of Beverly Hills contemplated a smoking ban for all its restaurants.

When the restaurateurs heard this, we joined forces and created the Beverly Hills Restaurant Association to fight the ban. I became the leader of the group and its first President.

Our argument wasn't that we were in favor of smoking, it was centered on the unfairness of the ordinance. We testified at the Beverly Hills City Council meeting that customers who smoked would go to restaurants in other cities where smoking was allowed; Beverly Hills restaurants would suffer.

Finally, the day of the vote came in 1987: the City of Beverly Hills' council voted to ban smoking in all restaurants with the exception of bars.

Exempting bars made it even worse for those restaurants that didn't have dining seating in their bars. The result of the smoking ban was predictable: people who smoked went to restaurants in the surrounding cities and the non-smokers didn't flock into the non-smoking restaurants. The business at The Grill went down 15 percent which was just about the amount of our profit margin. But we weren't the only ones affected; this happened to just about all the "fine dining" restaurants in Beverly Hills. This went on for about two months, which devastated the restaurants of Beverly Hills.

One night not long after the City Council passed the law, George Burns came in with an unlit cigar in his mouth and Allan pulled Burns' agent aside to remind him that smoking was no longer permitted, telling him, "I'm sorry but you can't let George light that cigar."

For the duration of the meal, Allan kept checking back in on their table, catching the eye of the agent to be sure that his famous client didn't light up. After dinner, George Burns put the unlit cigar back in his mouth and walked out into the middle of restaurant and started working all of the tables. Allan pulled Burns' agent aside again, pleading, "You've got to get him out of here before he lights that cigar!" Burns continued holding court and telling jokes to friends and patrons, all while holding his signature cigar between his thumb and forefinger at the corner of his mouth, unlit. When he finally reached the bar, George Burns took out a match, lit the cigar, and thanked Allan, before walking out into our alley to smoke.

I met with Beverly Hills Mayor Vicki Reynolds and Walt Borofsky, the head of the lobby group Americans for Nonsmokers' Rights, and the head of the American Lung Association. I told them if they would create a level playing field by adopting smoking and non-smoking sections in the city—like all the other restaurants in Los Angeles County—and sponsor a ban on smoking in *all* restaurants and bars in California, without any exemptions, I would be their spokesperson and support the ban.

Mayor Reynolds and the Beverly Hills City Council agreed to lift the smoking ban in Beverly Hills and adopt smoking and non-smoking sections. I kept my end of the bargain and they actually flew me and Leslie around the state to speak to city councils in support of a total ban on smoking in restaurants and bars. As a member of the California Restaurant Association, I went to the Association, which had 90 board members, and helped obtain a 46-44 vote in favor of supporting the statewide smoking ban by its members.

It took 10 years, but on January 1, 1998, California became the first state in the nation to ban smoking in all restaurants and bars. I was very proud of what Vicki and I had done to finally end smoking in all the bars and restaurants in California.

On the Map

The review that put us on the map, coast to coast, was by *New York Times* restaurant critic, Craig Claiborne, in January 1987.

At the time, Craig Claiborne was the most famous food critic in America, although I had never heard of him. Claiborne, the man who invented the four-star restaurant rating system, was a Southerner known for his exacting standards and extravagance. He came into town to do a couple of restaurant reviews and he was staying across the street at the Beverly Wilshire Hotel. When he was shopping on Rodeo and asked for a restaurant recommendation for lunch, they sent him to The Grill.

We were absolutely packed when he came in but when he told me he was a restaurant reviewer with the *New York Times*, I knew enough to get him a table. I went into the kitchen to tell John Sola that there was a food writer here but that I couldn't remember the guy's name. Sola asked, "Is it Craig Claiborne?"

I said, "Yeah, that's the one."

I wanted to point him out to John, but John didn't even want to know what table Claiborne was at; he just said, "Fine," and kept working. It was his consistency thing.

After lunch Craig Claiborne called me over and asked to meet with the chef. I went in the kitchen to get John, who asked me, "What did they have to eat?" He truly had no idea! I told him that Claiborne had eaten the Chicken Pot Pie, a daily special at the time, and his dining companion had ordered the corned beef hash. When John went to the table, Claiborne told him that it was the best pot pie and corned beef hash he had ever eaten.

Claiborne told John that he had to check with his editor, but that he wanted to fly him back to his East Hampton home for a cooking demonstration so the recipes could be published in the *New York Times Magazine*. A couple of days later, John got the call that Claiborne's editor had approved the trip and John made his travel arrangements. John had thought they told him to bring both the products and recipes for any ingredient that took more than two or three days to prepare (like the bordelaise sauce that he used in the corned beef hash), so he packed his suitcase with a freezer bag and some of his signature sauces.

Claiborne picked John up at the airport and drove him back to his home. He knew Scandia well and they chatted about Claiborne's favorite dishes there. When they arrived, Claiborne set John up in his kitchen with an assistant and told him, "I don't want you to chop, mix, dice or measure anything unless I'm in the room." Claiborne sat at one end of the counter with his typewriter while Sola was at the other end preparing the dishes. If he was using an onion, Claiborne would have Sola weigh the unpeeled onion, weigh the peeled and cleaned onion, and then weigh and measure the same diced onion. Sola had started making his chicken stock for the pot pie, and as he began unpacking his bag, he pulled out the freezer bag with the bordelaise sauce.

Craig Claiborne got very upset: "I said that everything has to be made here!" John told him that there must be a misunderstanding that the bordelaise sauce takes two to three days to make and he thought he was supposed to bring the product.

"I don't know if this going to work," Claiborne said, throwing his hands up in exasperation.

John said, "Don't worry, I'll make it work."

Claiborne had an extensive pantry and John pulled together a bunch of ingredients for the corned beef hash. Sweat started dripping down John's brow so Claiborne, still typing at the other end of the counter asked him, "Do you want a beer?" John happily accepted, hoping it would lighten the mood, but Claiborne immediately returned to his typewriter, scrutinizing and questioning every step, and occasionally muttering to himself in seeming frustration with John.

The demonstration for the two dishes lasted a grueling six hours. When John finally served Craig Claiborne the Chicken Pot Pie, Claiborne said, "Ah, just how I remembered it at The Grill." Then he told John, "Just wrap up the corned beef hash," and Claiborne stuck it in his freezer, at which point John figured he had failed the final exam.

When John returned to LA, everyone asked him how it went. "I don't know," he said. "It didn't start out very well. Then ten minutes later he gave me a beer. Then it didn't seem to end particularly well. So, I truly don't know."

The New Year's weekend of 1987, the *New York Times* Sunday Magazine came out featuring The Grill and had the recipe for The Grill's Chicken Pot Pie, which Claiborne called, "fabled." We were thrilled. Then several months later, totally unexpected, in an article on the perfect brunch, Claiborne published "John Sola's Corned Beef Hash" recipe in the *NY Times Magazine*. He wrote: "This hash takes some slicing and chopping, but it may be made well in advance and refrigerated. Or it may be made up to a month in advance and frozen." All I could picture was Craig Claiborne opening his freezer weeks after John had done the six-hour demonstration, stumbling upon the frozen corned beef hash, and reheating it in the microwave.

John had hit it out of the park. We were officially on the culinary map. The Chicken Pot Pie moved from a weekly special to a signature Grill dish, and remained a favorite three decades later. The Grill became a "must" destination for New Yorkers, tourists, and food-lovers coming to town.

Spago

One night in July 1988 we had a party of four sitting at table 32. Around 7 p.m. the server came to me; she had overheard her guests talking about the last night on their trip to Los Angeles. They had ordered The Grill's New York Pepper Steak which they had read about in *Gourmet* Magazine. They said the only restaurant on their list they were unable to eat at was Spago, which had the iconic Smoked Salmon Pizza.

I thought, let's make their trip a total success. I called Spago and told the hostess what I wanted to do and ordered the Smoked Salmon Pizza. I sent a busser over to pick it up and he returned just as our guests were finishing their meal. I went to the table and presented them with Spago's Smoked Salmon Pizza. They were so surprised! They tried to hand me a $100 bill but I refused. I told them to take care of the busser who ran to Spago to pick up the pizza.

They bought a $160 bottle of Cristal Champaign and insisted I sit and have a glass with them—which I did. They were in the oil and gas business in Denver, Colorado. I asked them which restaurants they had visited while on their trip. They listed: Morton's, Lawry's, Trumps, and The Gril on the Alley. I asked why they didn't go to Spago and they told me they couldn't get a reservation. I told them if they wanted to stay one more night, I'd call Wolfgang Puck and get them a reservation. They were most appreciative, but they had to get back home. As they left The Grill, they could not have been happier. Giving the guest what they want—even if it wasn't from our restaurant—was what made The Grill so special and still in demand after 40 years in business.

The President Is Coming

Monday, November 6, 1989, the Secret Service called. President Ronald Reagan was coming to the restaurant for lunch the next day with a party of seven people. I was to have a booth in the corner for the President and his party, with two separate tables flanking the booth where the Secret Service agents would sit. The Secret Service would be in that afternoon to check the table arrangements. I was cautioned not to *breathe a word* about this visit to *anyone*. I told nobody...except Leslie. That afternoon three agents arrived to check out the restaurant. When they left, I was again cautioned not to tell anyone.

The next day at 12:30 p.m. the President of the United States arrived with his entourage. As soon as the President walked in a hush came over the room. This reaction was common when a big celebrity came in. Then everyone in the dining room stood up and gave President Reagan a standing ovation. That has never happened before or since.

When the President's party was seated at booth 133, I was called over to another table. The guest who called me over told me he was the wine maker at Jordan Vineyard & Winery. We bought a lot of wine from his company, so I knew who he was. He said the White House always poured Jordan Cabernet and Chardonnay at the State dinners and he wanted to buy the President's table a bottle of wine. I went over to the President's table to let him know the wine was compliments of Jordan Vineyard & Winery and would he like a Cabernet or Chardonnay? He looked at me with a blank stare, as though he didn't understand what I was asking. I then said, "Red or white, Mr. President?" He seemed flustered so I asked him what he was going to eat. He told me he was going to have a grilled cheese sandwich; I selected a chardonnay.

After the server took their order, Izzy, our broiler-man, called me into the kitchen to let me know the exhaust fan was broken and the kitchen was filling up with smoke! I momentarily panicked, and then did what any other restaurateur would do: I ran up to the attic and climbed the ladder to the roof where the exhaust equipment was located. At least I knew that much! I pulled the cover off the unit; the motor was silent. It wasn't running. I'm not sure what I expected but that's what I saw. I hurried back down the stairs.

My next worry was that the fire suppression system would get hot and dispense the white powder fire-retardant chemical all over the kitchen and into the dining room. I was afraid at that point the Secret Service would think it was a cocaine bust and shoot someone—probably me!

We opened all the doors in the kitchen and everyone grabbed flattened cardboard boxes and manually fanned the smoke out of the room for the duration of lunch. Luckily, nothing happened and the rest of the lunch went without a hitch.

When it was time for the President to leave, he stood up and the entire dining room also rose and applauded. President Reagan put one hand in his pocket and waved to the diners with the other. That day, our staff also deserved a standing ovation for pulling off a flawless lunch service despite the drama in the kitchen.

President Reagan walked out of the restaurant to a crowd of about 500 people that had gathered, waiting for a chance to see him. He again put one hand in his pocket and waived to the crowd. There was a woman with a baby standing close to him. He took the baby from the woman, kissed the baby, and handed him back to the mother, then slid into a waiting limousine.

I wondered how all those people standing outside knew he was there. After all, the only person I had told was Leslie, and she wouldn't tell anyone. Well, it seems *The Hollywood Reporter* ran a story that morning that the President was having lunch at The Grill. I guess his marketing department gave out the story. That was one of the most exciting days at The Grill.

My Kind of Celebrity

Another night, Bob Uecker came into the restaurant. Uecker was a former Major League Baseball player, a regular on the Johnny Carson show, and was in a television series titled "Mr. Belvedere" between 1985 and 1990. He and his agent, who worked for William Morris Talent Agency, would sit at the bar just about every night they were taping the show. (He loved the Joe's Special, a scramble of ground beef, spinach and eggs that came from Original Joe's in San Francisco.) I came to know him quite well and Leslie and I would go out to dinner with Bob and his wife, Judy.

One night while Bob was sitting at the bar, Stan Musial, one of the five most famous baseball players in the 1960s, came into the restaurant. "Uke" had played with him, and they knew each other. "Stan the Man" as he was known, sat down at the bar with Uke, took a harmonica out of the lapel pocket of his jacket and started playing tunes while Uke and I sang along. Everyone in the restaurant gathered around to listen. It was a very exciting night for me. I had always wanted to be a baseball player and here I had two famous players sitting at our bar.

Celebrations

In 1994, Fred Hayman sold Georgio, the fragrance, to Procter and Gamble. He also owned the Giorgio Boutique on the corner of Rodeo and Dayton Way next door to The Grill. Since the sale, he could no longer use the name "Giorgio" for his store, so he changed it to Beverly Hills 273, which was the store's address.

Fred wanted to have a major party to announce the new name. He rented the Warner Bros. Pictures lot in Hollywood Hills and invited 1,000 people to celebrate the new store. He had his five favorite restaurants cater the event: Spago, Chasen's, The Bistro, Jimmy's, and The Grill on the Alley. These five restaurants were considered the finest in Los Angeles and we were more than proud to be part of this illustrious group.

While we were all setting up for the party that night, we saw a skunk enter the tent in the area where the guests' coats were to be checked during the event. Nobody could find the skunk. Meanwhile, the guests were checking their expensive mink coats. Well, the skunk did what skunks do. I think the cleaning bill was as much as the cost of the party.

In 1996, Fred had another party to celebrate his marriage to Bette. A year in advance he had checked the almanac to see when, in August 1996, there would be a full moon. Fred picked that date and went about planning the party of the decade. It would be held on his property in Malibu on a bluff about 50 feet above the Pacific Ocean. The same five favorite restaurants catered for the party and he set up an outdoor kitchen for each of the restaurants. We cooked Prime New York Steaks and served them on a round, sourdough roll with natural gravy and creamed horseradish. We also served a Caesar Salad, a specialty of The Grill.

Fred met with the staff before the celebration to let them

know he had ordered pizza and salad for the crew. This was very generous as the individual restaurants would normally be responsible for providing staff meals. Fred wanted everyone working at the event to have enough to eat but he also let them know that under no circumstances was anyone to be seen eating behind their stations when the party was going on.

After the party was in full swing and all guests had eaten, Fred called everyone together on the lawn where 100 gospel singers were assembled and sang "America the Beautiful" as the full moon rose over the Pacific Ocean. At this time, a barge pulled into view and put on the most beautiful fireworks show. The show ended with "I Love You Bette" spelled out in fireworks. This was Fred's way of celebrating their anniversary.

Hector's Brooches

Not only did people come to The Grill to see Hollywood celebrities, they also came to see team members, who became "celebrities" in their own way. Hector Camacho was the first server hired at The Grill on the Alley and in 2015 became the maître d' on Thursday, Friday, and Saturday nights. Hector has always been very popular with guests and now that he was working the front door, people would come to the restaurant just to see him.

Hector always wore a beautiful suit and tie accompanied by a unique accessory on the lapel: an antique brooch. Guests took notice and would bring Hector brooches, many from their own collections and some that had been in their families for over 100 years and share their stories about the ornament.

Steve Lawrence, husband and singing partner of the late Eydie Gorme, brought in a beautiful pin of a man and woman dancing, their diamond-studded legs shimmering. "Eydie would have loved for you to have this brooch," he told Hector.

To date, Hector has over 500 brooches brought in by The Grill's guests. He keeps a list of all the pins and who gave them to him. When one of these special guests has a reservation, Hector makes sure he is wearing their brooch.

Chapter 13
The Daily Grill

The Grill on the Alley in Beverly Hills was very successful. We had been open four-and-a-half years, and nobody had tried to copy our concept – yet. Perhaps the time was right to establish another restaurant.

As part of my contract with The Grill, I was allowed to leave and work on other restaurants once all the investors had been repaid in full, and on the condition that I continued to manage The Grill for its first five years. I had a big decision to make: should Leslie and I build a restaurant alone or do it with Mike and Richard? I knew if we were going to do it with partners, we'd have to open several restaurants. If Leslie and I did it alone, one more restaurant would be enough to support us.

After thinking long and hard, I decided to proceed with my partners, more out of loyalty than anything else. I loved The Grill and didn't want to break up the partnership. We decided that rather than raise the money to open one more restaurant we would set up a corporation, Grill Concepts, Inc. (GCI), that could open several restaurants under the same trade name. The new restaurant concept would be a less expensive version of The Grill on the Alley.

Leslie found a location on the second floor of a three-story strip mall in Brentwood, about two miles from our home and three miles from The Grill. Now, I would normally avoid a second-floor location. People usually shop on the first floor and only venture to the second floor if there's a store they want to go to. The landlord, however, wanted restaurants on the second floor to draw people there, which would make the second floor more popular with retail stores and therefore, easier to lease. Because of this, the landlord gave us a much better rent deal than we would have gotten on the first floor, along with $75,000 to help with the construction.

That being said, I was still worried about being the only restaurant on the second floor so I went to Larry Flax and Rick Rosenfield, the owners of a new concept restaurant called California Pizza Kitchen (CPK) and asked if they would like to have a location on the second floor in the same center. CPK served "designer" pizzas; their specialty was a barbeque chicken pizza. The cuisine was different enough that it wouldn't compete with our menu, and they attracted the same client demographic: upper middle-class with sophisticated tastes and disposable income. I felt the two concepts would be quite compatible and create more of a draw to the second floor. This would be a second restaurant for CPK. They agreed and we became neighbors.

Now we had to come up with a name for our new restaurant. Everyone had a different idea. Richard liked The Pine Grill. I favored Joe's Grill as a nod to my father's Smokey Joe's restaurants where I started working as a boy. Even Larry Flax had a name he loved: The Minute Grill. Finally, Leslie came up with the perfect name: Daily Grill. The idea behind the name was that the menu was so large, you could eat there every day. Everyone loved it and we adopted the name Daily Grill.

We hired a General Manager by the name of Maggie Radzwiller who was an accomplished chef and possessed a background in restaurant operations, a rare combination. She wrote our training manual and employment policies and procedures.

Next, we needed to discuss how to raise the money to open the restaurant. GCI would raise the necessary capital and we sold shares in the corporation. Our plans were to open several Daily Grills. We hired award-winning architect Steve Ehrlich and Richard worked closely with Steve to develop a design which cost significantly less to execute than The Grill in Beverly Hills.

The new restaurant would be less expensive to build and operate. It would have the "feel" of an American Grill, but on a more moderate scale. We would use vinyl floors (The Grill had marble), acoustical tile ceilings (The Grill had an intricate, wood coffer ceiling), smaller booths and chairs to maximize seating per square foot, bare walls, and less expensive furniture. The décor, design, and restrooms were much simpler. We would use white paper on top of a white tablecloth, making it possible to use the same tablecloths for every seating during the day. Many of the table set ups were the same; however, we would use stainless steel cutlery instead of the silver-plated tableware used at The Grill.

The service would be modified for maximum efficiency. At The Grill, we used two servers for every 20 guests; the new restaurant would have one server for every 18 guests. Rather than have the servers also bringing the food to the table, we used food runners to serve the food, which freed our servers to wait on the guests.

The new restaurant would not take reservations, which allowed for more efficient seating and eliminated having to hold tables until the reservation arrived. We also didn't have to worry about "no shows" which was a big problem in those days. "No shows" were people who had a reservation, didn't cancel, and didn't show up.

Many of the food items and portions were the same as offered at The Grill, but the average meal cost per person was about 40 percent lower. A lot of The Grill check average differences had to do with a full bar and high-priced wine by the bottle. The new restaurant would serve beer and wine by the glass only. All in all, while The Grill on the Alley was a fine dining experience, the Daily Grill would serve a great meal without the full dining experience or expense.

The menu was similar, but where The Grill's Shrimp Cocktail had five very large shrimp, the Daily Grill used smaller and less expensive bay shrimp. The beef we used for all the steaks at the Daily Grill was Certified Angus Choice; The Grill on the Alley used USDA Prime. John Sola, the original chef of The Grill, oversaw the kitchen at the Daily Grill as well. He did all the hiring and training of the kitchen staff for three weeks before opening. Maggie and I did the dining room hiring and training for two weeks before opening.

Before opening, we had a trial run by inviting people for meals. On the Friday before opening, we had 40 people for breakfast, lunch, and dinner. On that Saturday, we had 80 people for all three meal periods, and on Sunday we had 120 people for each of the three meal periods. This trial run gave us a chance to work through any problems before officially opening. After three days of preparing and serving breakfasts, lunches, and dinners, we would usually be ready to open.

On Monday, we gave everyone the day off and then on Tuesday, September 27, 1988, we opened the doors at 7 a.m. to a waiting line of people.

Breakfast was slow that first day but at lunch, the entire restaurant filled up in the first hour and we served 270 people. Dinner was the same with hour-long waits from 5 p.m. to 10 p.m. Unlike The Grill in Beverly Hills, we didn't have the luxury of the first two weeks being slow. The Daily Grill only had 90 seats and we never expected to be that busy! The first seating went well, but with the second seating, we started to have some problems.

In a restaurant, food has to be prepped ahead of time. There are sauces to be made, hamburger meat to be ground and made into hamburger patties, steaks and seafood need to be cut to proper sizes, and vegetables need to be cleaned, peeled, and cut.

Take the Cobb salad, for instance. There are eight ingredients to this salad. The chicken must be poached and diced, the blue cheese chipped off a block and made into crumbles, the bacon fried and crumbled, the vegetables cut, etc. This all takes time.

Menu cover from the Daily Grill, Brentwood, CA

We would prepare enough food for one-and-a-half times what we were estimating business to be, but the Daily Grill was a new venture, and we didn't have a track record yet. We based our food prep on 90 seats so we prepared enough food for 150 people. That might be enough for two seatings but by the beginning of the third seating we were running out of food. I made the decision to close the restaurant at 3 p.m. and reopen at 6 to give the team a little rest before dinner. By 6 p.m. there was a line of over 100 people waiting for dinner. I couldn't seat everyone at once because the servers wouldn't be able to take all the orders so I decided to seat the first six parties and wait 10 minutes before seating the second group of six parties, at which time the restaurant would be full. That worked quite well so we continued the policy for the rest of the week. This gave us a little breathing room.

I decided to close the restaurant for a few hours and re-open at 5:30 p.m. During those two hours, John and his team prepped for dinner, which was a separate menu from lunch service. The entire day shift from The Grill on the Alley in Beverly Hills came over and worked until 9 p.m., cutting and prepping for dinner. The night cooks had to work until 3 a.m. to get ready for lunch the next day.

All this time, Chef John Sola had been at the Daily Grill since 6 a.m. Without him, we never would have been able to open the next day. John went home at 3 a.m. and came back to the restaurant at 7 a.m. to get started again. Maggie and I were also there from 6 a.m. to 10 p.m. We had planned for 100 lunches and 100 dinners the first day; we did 600 covers (meals) total. The same thing happened the rest of the week. Fortunately, we were closed on Sunday, which gave us all time to regroup.

That Sunday, John, Maggie, and I got together to plan for the second week. We realized the only way we were going to get all the food prepped for the next day was if we had a prep crew working all night.

As John and I talked about who would lead this effort, we came up with the name at the same time: "Chef Ahmet." We had previously interviewed him for the head chef's position but didn't hire him because, at the time, we didn't feel we needed a chef with his credentials. We called and told him he had a job. He needed to bring in five prep cooks and start at 10 p.m. that night. We gave him a list of vegetables, potatoes, meats, and cheeses to cut for breakfast and lunch. He had to get his work done by seven in the morning, at which time the breakfast and lunch crew would come in and do the prepping for that day's lunch and dinner. This process would happen six days a week. We continued using the overnight prep crew for about six weeks until we learned how to handle the business. Chef Ahmet and his overnight prep crew saved us.

Each day we opened at 7 a.m. for breakfast, which was usually calm. However, at about 11:30 a.m. there were 100 or so people waiting in line to sit down for lunch. We had 20 tables and 15 counter seats in the restaurant: six servers covered the tables, and one server was behind the counter.

I couldn't seat all the tables at 11:30 a.m. because the servers could only greet one table at a time to explain the menu, get beverages, take lunch orders, and enter the order into the computer, at which time the cooks would start preparing their meals. Therefore, I could only seat six of the parties at a time. I would wait six or seven minutes and seat the next six tables then wait another 10 minutes to seat the remaining tables. By that time, it was almost noon and we had a half-hour wait already. By 12:45 p.m., the wait was one hour, and it stayed that way until about 3 p.m. when we would close for two hours to prepare for dinner. We were serving 800 people a day, the maximum our 20 tables and 15 counter seats could handle. The rest of the week, we continued to serve about 800 meals a day and the all-night prepping crew was barely able to keep up.

On Saturday the Daily Grill was open for brunch. The brunch menu featured several omelets including "design your own" which allowed guests to choose their omelet ingredients.

That first Saturday we opened at 9 a.m. to a waiting line of about 25 people. We seated everyone and off we went.

The first table ordered five omelets. All the tables seated ordered at least two omelets. As the omelets were made, the servers delivered them to the tables. Now we had an issue. People would cut into their omelet, only to find out it wasn't what they ordered. We did not have a system to identify what was inside the omelets! They would send the meal back, and we would have to make all new omelets. This happened with all the tables who ordered omelets at our first seating.

We realized we had to mark each omelet so the servers could identify what was in them. This was accomplished by putting a small amount of the ingredients on top of the cooked omelet. This worked fine, but it took over an hour to redo all the omelets that came back. Our first brunch was a total disaster! The wait line grew longer and ran into the lunch menu which ran into the dinner menu. After about three weeks, the weekday breakfasts slowed down. Lunches, dinners, and weekend brunches continued to be crazy.

Leslie and I lived in Brentwood and between all the people she already knew plus the people she had met at The Grill, she knew about half of the guests coming into the Daily Grill. Leslie is a very engaging person and her interactions with people waiting for tables was helpful for the business those first few weeks. Without her mingling and talking to those waiting in line, half of the guests would have given up and walked out.

I talked with Mike and Richard, and we came up with a plan. I then went to Chef John Sola and said, "I have good news and bad news. The good news is we are going to close for breakfast. The bad news is we are going to open Sundays." I explained it's hard to have a restaurant called the Daily Grill and then be closed one day a week. He was disappointed but understood,

139

although he thought the restaurant needed one down day. A six-day work week is much easier to schedule because you just have to give everyone one additional day off each week instead of two days.

John grew tired as the days went on at this unrelenting pace. One night during the third week I found John on the back porch, leaning over the railing, his face in his hands. He said, "I just can't do it anymore." I encouraged him to go home and get a good night's rest and we would talk about it tomorrow. He did and was back at 8 a.m. the next day.

By the fourth week, Chef John Sola was working 18 hours a day; he was burned out. I tried to get him as much help as I could, but his work ethic was such that he insisted on being at the restaurant all the hours we were open.

In appreciation for how hard he worked, we gave John two tickets to the first game of the 1988 World Series (October 15) game at Dodger Stadium between the Dodgers and the Oakland Athletics. This was the game where Kirk Gibson hit what is called "the most famous home run in Dodger History." Gibson had injuries to both legs and wasn't expected to even play when he was called up to pinch hit. The Dodgers were trailing 4-3 and had two outs in the bottom of the ninth inning and a tying run at first base. Gibson's home run helped the Dodgers defeat the Oakland A's; it was Gibson's only time at bat during that World Series. John went to the game; however, he left early because he was so tired and never saw the "most famous" home run.

I had been spending most of my time at the Daily Grill. Fortunately, The Grill in Beverly Hills had a great management team. Israel Camacho and Neil Roth were the kitchen managers. Allan Ludwig and Jeffrey Best managed the dining room, and Donna Sloate and her assistant Jeff Cleveland ran the office and answered the phones. Also, Leslie would go by

The Grill every evening and let me know what was going on. This strong team gave me the time to run the Daily Grill without worrying about The Grill on the Alley.

Part of the success of the Daily Grill was our attention to details. Chef John Sola, Maggie, and I worked on every aspect of the restaurant. The coffee beans were ground for every fresh pot of coffee; however, the coffee taste was inconsistent. We worked with Howard Gordon, our coffee bean supplier, and learned that the beans we were using, although they were of a very fine quality, were quite oily. This was typical of freshly roasted coffee beans but the oiliness caused them to get stuck in the hopper which caused the machine to dispense irregular amounts of ground coffee which caused the taste to be inconsistent. Howard convinced us to buy the coffee in pre-measured, vacuum-sealed aluminum bags for maximum consistency. This solved the problem without changing the taste of every brew.

Another issue was that only Chef John Sola knew how to butcher the veal for the Piccata and Marsala recipes, and this took a bit of time. We switched from veal to chicken for these recipes which allowed us to sell the chicken for about half the price we had to charge for the veal. This also considerably reduced the prepping time.

The sixth week the Daily Grill was open, Chef John Sola came to me—he was going to quit. He had decided to move back to Lake Tahoe and open his own restaurant. This was a terrible blow to me, but I knew it was the best thing for him. By this time, I had a friend, Toni Hipp, a very fine European-trained chef, helping us out. Toni had just closed his restaurant in Beverly Hills. I offered Toni the Executive Chef job and he accepted. The next four weeks, Toni trained under John and in late November of 1988, was in charge of both The Grill on the Alley and the Daily Grill kitchens.

By this time, it was our third month in business, and we had grown into the volume of the Daily Grill, which for the most part, was running smoothly. The Grill in Beverly Hills continued to maintain the standard our guests had come to expect. I now had two restaurants; two dreams come true.

The Grill on the Alley, 1990. Left to right: Toni Hipp, Bob Spivak, Leslie Spivak, John Sola

About six months after opening Daily Grill, Maggie decided to get married and move to San Francisco. We were sad to see her go as our plan was to open more restaurants and have Maggie go along with us. We had a very loyal team member by the name of Katie Revitz who had worked for my father at the Bouillabaisse and was the General Manager at the Daily Grill in Brentwood. (A few years later, we promoted Marla Bornstein from Newport Beach Daily Grill to be part of Katie's management team. Later, both Marla and Katie would become intricate members of the team as our company grew.)

At about that time, we started looking for a second Daily Grill location and found an ideal spot in a new shopping center at La Cienega and Beverly boulevards about two miles west of The Grill on the Alley in Beverly Hills. The center was building a state-of-the-art movie theater along with several restaurants, boutique shops, and what would be the largest book and record store in Los Angeles County. More importantly, there was plenty of parking.

To sign that lease, GCI had to raise more money. We gave the investors 10 percent ownership in the company for the first restaurant. With the success of the first Daily Grill, we were able to raise the money to open two more restaurants and offer an additional five percent ownership in the corporation.

We had a husband-and-wife team who were very good servers at the Brentwood location. They trained the new opening team for the La Cienega location using Maggie's service training manual as a guide. The Daily Grill La Cienega was a triple-A location. In a three-mile radius of this location was the most densely populated residential area west of New York City. It had all the demographics we could want. The lunch business came from the working neighborhood. In addition to the daytime shoppers, we also had the largest hospital, Cedars Sinai Medical Center, within walking distance. For dinner, we had a strong residential population plus the shoppers and movie-goers from the Beverly Center.

The restaurant was much larger than the first Daily Grill. While the Brentwood location seated 90 people, the La Cienega location seated about 150. The opening was very strong, and with the additional seating and our experience with the first Daily Grill, we were able to serve about 1,000 covers a day after the third week.

This location had a side door located close to the restrooms that led directly to the parking lot, which would be a convenient exit for guests. Conventional wisdom would be to make this a Fire Exit only as people could say they were going to the restroom and then walk out this side door without paying for their meal. I decided to make this a proper exit because I didn't want to penalize the honest guests by making them go to the front door and walk around the whole building to get to the parking lot. I told the team that if this became a problem, we would reconsider. No one ever used this exit to skip out on a bill.

This Daily Grill became our highest volume restaurant and set the stage for us to expand to Newport Beach.

Chapter 14
Turning a Company of Restaurants into a Restaurant Company

After opening the second Daily Grill at La Cienega and Beverly boulevards in Los Angeles, we signed a lease to open in Newport Beach in a large upscale shopping mall called Fashion Island. Newport Beach was an hour from Los Angeles, but the normal heavy traffic could make it a two-hour commute. Since I would be spending a lot of time there prior to the opening, Leslie and I rented an apartment close to the new location.

We were in the early stages of getting the location ready when Chef John Sola called and said he was coming to Los Angeles. Leslie and I invited him to our house for dinner; I would cook. That evening, John told me he never did open his own restaurant; he just needed to get away.

"You need to be back with your family," I said, and that night John agreed to move back to Los Angeles and start working with our company again. This was the best thing that could have happened to us! I didn't think it was fair to replace Toni, so I told John he would start as the opening chef at the new Newport Beach restaurant. He agreed and now we had the greatest chef back in the fold.

Next, we needed to hire someone with strong corporate experience. I thought of Chuck Frank. Chuck and I had been on a panel for the California Restaurant Association. Chuck had been CFO of Spectrum Restaurants, a company which owned 12 different restaurants in San Francisco and Los Angeles. When Spectrum sold to a large restaurant company, Chuck became President and Chief Operating Officer but later decided to leave and go into the restaurant consulting business. I contacted

Chuck to see if he could help me.

Chuck lived near San Francisco but traveled to Los Angeles every other week to work with Johnny Rockets, a small four-unit restaurant company selling hamburgers and malts. Chuck said he could spend a day with me as well. Chuck's wife, Barbara, had told him he was spending too much time in the house and that she "had married him for better or worse, but not for lunch." Therefore, spending two days every other week in Los Angeles worked out just fine. Johnny Rockets was having the same growing pains problem we were having.

Chuck worked with me to develop the necessary systems and manuals needed to turn a company of restaurants into a unified restaurant company. When he came to Los Angeles, he stayed at our house. Chuck continued working with us for more than 10 years and we became very good friends. We always said if we ever both retired, we'd make a good consulting team.

The opening of the Newport Beach Daily Grill was very busy, but after three months it started to slow down. This was the first of our four restaurants that began having sales problems and we suspected it had something to do with the physical location which was in a quiet corner of the mall.

You had to want to find the restaurant; there wasn't a lot of foot traffic. Because of this, the mall gave us a very large tenant improvement allowance (TI) and low rent, which, financially, made it much less costly to open. Later, we realized the large TI was due to the out-of-the-way location. Despite this, I believed the Daily Grill was so good that once people found us, they would tell others and word-of-mouth would carry the day. A redeeming factor was the restaurant was near the mall's parking lot, which we thought would be an asset once people found us. The restaurant made money and stayed at the location for a long time but was not a big hit like the others. To this day, I wonder why.

After three months in Newport Beach, I gave up the apartment and returned to Los Angeles. One of the most important things in a restaurant is consistency, and yet, in just the three short months I'd been away, things had changed at The Grill and the two Daily Grills in Brentwood and La Cienega.

When recipes and policies are not documented, other people put their spin on them and the result doesn't resemble what you started with. It's almost like the game of Telephone we played when we were kids where you lined up seven or eight kids and the person at the head of the line whispered a secret to the person next to them and they repeated it to the next person in line and so on. The person at the end of the line would say what he or she heard, and it rarely resembled the secret told by the first person. The same thing happens to recipes and policies when the information is not reinforced on a daily basis. That's when I knew we needed to document everything.

Chuck and John Sola created a recipe book. Chuck also worked with Louie Feinstein, our Director of Operations, to establish an employee ("team member") handbook documenting all the rules, policies, and procedures. We also computerized the accounting systems.

One of my pet peeves is when the service person doesn't know who ordered what food item. I would call it a "food auction." You know who had the hamburger so the remaining dishes are served by process of elimination or asking "who had what." With our new Team Member handbook, we were able to address this problem with a simple number system.

If there were six people at a table, the server would write the numbers one through six on the order pad. The person facing the front door was automatically given the number one position. The server would then proceed clockwise around the table, taking orders and writing each order next to the corresponding number. When they entered the order on the computer, there was a place to add the guest number along with the order. When the server brought the food to the table, they would start by serving person number one and then work their way around the table. You don't expect to see this at a casual dining restaurant, but you certainly expect the server to deliver the correct order at a fine dining restaurant. Just documenting a policy isn't enough to provide change; you had to have management reinforce the policies on a daily basis.

From a guest perspective, receiving the correct meal from the server is just one of several ways guests subconsciously judge the restaurant. The guest experience is made up of a myriad of subliminal messages. A smudged door, a crooked picture on the wall, a lamp with a burned-out lightbulb, or tables stacked with dirty dishes—a guest may notice all these things before they even taste the food. If the server takes three minutes to approach the table, doesn't smile, and has a dirty apron, but does everything else right and the food is great, the guest may still leave with an unfavorable opinion about the restaurant without ever really being able to identify exactly why. The negative subliminal details made the decision for them.

As an example, Leslie made a reservation at a new "hot" restaurant. The person taking her reservation said, "Don't be late. We only hold the table for 10 minutes." They were nice about it, but you can't tell someone that without creating a negative subliminal message. We arrived 10 minutes early. I walked in, gave the person at the desk my name and said we had a 6 p.m. reservation. That person told us we were 10 minutes early and had to wait until 6 p.m. before we could be seated.

I said, "No problem. We'll just sit over here and wait." The host said, "You can't sit there until we open."

This didn't seem right to me, so I said, "Let me get this straight. If I'm 10 minutes late, you give my table away. If I'm

10 minutes early, I must wait in my car. Is that correct?"

"Yes, that's correct," they replied.

Well, this could have been the best dining experience of my life but there was no way I was going to like this restaurant. As it turned out, everything else was great. However, we never went back, and I had forgotten about the restaurant until one day I read in the newspaper they were closing. I sort of smiled when I read that. *No wonder they didn't make it with the attitude they showed me at the door!*

I always teach our people the importance of strict attention to detail. My eyes are trained to see all these things when I walk into a restaurant. If there is a light bulb out, or anything else that can be perceived as a negative, we take care of it. That attention to detail is why I believe our restaurants have been so successful.

Encino developer Michael Pache was developing Encino Place, a mall with an outside escalator to the second floor like the Brentwood Center where the first Daily Grill was located. Michael contacted us with a deal we couldn't turn down: his offer provided enough money to build the restaurant and purchase all the kitchen equipment, dining room fixtures, and tables and chairs. It was a turn-key deal. We said yes and built the fourth Daily Grill in Encino.

The Daily Grill was a big draw doing about 600 covers a day. That meant 600 people, every day, came to Encino Place to eat at the Daily Grill. This level of foot traffic enabled the developer to attract more retail stores. Michael also made the same deal with California Pizza Kitchen, which brought in another 500 people a day. CPK and Daily Grill replicated the synergy created from their first pairing in Brentwood. One day people would come to the center for pizza and another day they would come for our American food menu.

One of my favorite team members at the Encino Daily Grill was a young man named Freddy. He started as a busser and quickly became a food runner, bringing food to the table when the server was busy. Everyone loved Freddy.

One day, Freddy didn't show up for work. He later called — from jail. The police had stopped him on his way home the previous night for a broken taillight. Freddy was a former gang kid who had a police record. He was arrested and we had to get him out of jail the next day. The police never pressed charges. Shortly after that incident, Freddy was promoted to waiter. Every time I would come into the Encino restaurant, I'd ask for Freddy. I truly had a soft spot in my heart for him.

We used to hire "mystery shoppers" to come into the restaurant as regular guests and then write a report documenting their dining experience. All the reports would come to me. Well, one shopper reported a terrible experience at the Encino restaurant. The server greeted the table on time, took their order, and then the trouble began. After the mystery shopper gave their order to the server, they waited for 45 minutes without getting their food. They called the server over and asked what was taking so long. The server responded, "The fucking manager didn't schedule enough cooks."

I looked at the name of the server and sure enough, it was Freddy. I smiled and thought if anyone was going to get caught saying something like that it had to be Freddy.

I went over to the restaurant and privately met with him and explained he couldn't talk to our guests like that. Freddy apologized and told me it would never happen again. I told him I would not say anything to his manager; it was just between us.

Several years later I was talking to the restaurant's General Manager and happened to ask if Freddy was still there. He said Freddy had quit and no longer worked for the company. When

I asked if he left on good terms, the manager said, yes, he gave one month's notice and left on good terms with everyone who worked there.

I asked the manager if he knew how to get in touch with Freddy and he told me some of the team members kept in touch with him. I requested that the next time someone had contact with Freddy to ask him to call me.

Freddy called a few months later. I asked how he was doing and what he was doing. He told me he was working for UPS in their warehouses. I told him that if he ever needed to talk with someone, he could come and see me. A few weeks later Freddy called, and we made plans to meet at a coffee shop across the street from my office at 3 p.m.

The day came and I arrived at the coffee shop on time and waited for Freddy. Three-thirty came, and still no Freddy. I waited another 15 minutes and then returned to my office. I called his former manager at the Encino Daily Grill and told him Freddy had stood me up, but that if he heard from him, to give me a call.

When Freddy finally did call, I asked what happened. He told me he didn't leave enough time to get to the meeting and when he realized he was going to be late, he was embarrassed, so he just went home. I asked him if he wanted to meet again to call me, and he did. We met, he was on time, and we talked about his life, his job, and other personal topics. I continued to meet with him once a week for several weeks. I told him if he ever wanted to come back, I would get him in a management training program at the Daily Grill. I told him he had to make sure he was ready for this as he only had one chance.

He called a few weeks later and said he was ready to make the move into management. Freddy came back to work for us and was a successful manager for two years. Then he was offered a better opportunity at another restaurant. He called me and I told him he should take the other job. He was very successful at the new restaurant and met a wonderful young woman who was a schoolteacher, and they got married. The last time we talked, he was moving to South Carolina where his wife's parents lived. I felt like my faith in him was warranted. Freddy turned his life around and I'm sure he is doing fine to this day.

Our fifth Daily Grill opened in July 1993 in Studio City, about five miles east of Encino. A developer building the same kind of shopping center as Encino Place offered the same deal structure we had in Encino. We were on the second floor and this location also had an outdoor escalator like both Brentwood and Encino. This was an excellent location, and the restaurant did about one-third more business than the Encino Daily Grill in a very similar facility. The difference between Encino and Studio City was the density of the residential community and proximity to CBS Studio Center, the television and movie production studios. Encino had very strong household incomes, much greater than Studio City, in fact, but they didn't have the density of Studio City. There were very few apartments in Encino. All the great wealth lived-in single-family homes on very large properties. Studio City had more high-end apartment units. Also, we did a lot of business with CBS and Warner Bros. studios.

As we were building the location, I applied for a liquor license. All of our restaurants had liquor licenses and I never had a problem with the Alcohol Beverage Control Board. This time, the neighborhood residents' association filed an objection to our license. It seems the neighborhood didn't want the shopping center to be built. They appealed everything the new center applied for. They lost all their appeals and objecting to our license was their last chance to have control on who the tenants were going to be. We were just about ready to open and

I needed to have the liquor license approved. I talked to Ira Smedra, the owner of the center, and let him know I wanted to speak with the residents' association to plead our case. I told Ira he should not attend the meeting; the residents had hard feelings against him because he had won all the appeals and built the center. I asked him to let me deal with them.

I went to the meeting and was friendly with all the group. I told them I understood how they disliked having the new center in their neighborhood, but the reality was there is going to be a shopping center. I explained we were a nice family restaurant which would be a benefit to their neighborhood. If they were successful in stopping us from getting the liquor license they would end up with a McDonald's or some other fast-food concept that didn't need a liquor license. They needed to make the choice. They couldn't argue with my logic and voted overwhelmingly to approve our liquor application without holding a hearing. We opened on time and judging by our tremendous sales the first few weeks, the neighborhood loved the restaurant.

While we were building Studio City, we signed our sixth Daily Grill location in Palm Desert, about eight miles east of Palm Springs in the Coachella Valley. The Palm Desert Daily Grill opened in January of 1994 and was the busiest opening since Brentwood. It was just crazy! People waited two hours for a table. The locals would come in expecting special seating attention and we had to tell them it was "first come, first serve." That wasn't very well received, and they let us know that come summer, when the seasonal trade disappeared and we would need their business, they wouldn't come in because we wouldn't give them special attention in season. There wasn't anything we could do about this. That was our policy.

Well, when summer came our business dropped from $100,000 a week to $20,000 a week. All the money we made in the winter was lost in the summer. It was awful. The residents wouldn't come in.

Our management team came up with a plan for the next season. We decided to start the Coachella Valley Residents Association. You had to have a Coachella Valley address to become part of the association and if you were a member during the season, you could phone ahead, provide your association number, and find out how long the wait would be. Their name would go on the wait list and a table would be ready within 10 minutes of their arrival. This worked great and the locals really appreciated it. Also, in the summer we mailed fliers to the members, offering a free item each month. One month might be free lemonade, another month might be a free appetizer or dessert. The following summer our sales doubled to a reasonable $40,000 a week. This ultimately became our busiest Daily Grill in California.

On January 17, 1994, the Northridge earthquake hit Los Angeles. Leslie and I were staying in a hotel in Palm Desert and the earthquake was so powerful that when it hit at 4:30 a.m., the whole room shook. We jumped out of bed. Although we were 100 miles from the epicenter, we still felt a strong jolt. We called our kids, and all were well, but still, we rushed home to see if any damage occurred, leaving the Palm Desert Daily Grill to the management. Fortunately, our home had very little damage. Some things fell over but that was about all. Pretty amazing when you consider that our house in Los Angeles was only 10 miles from the epicenter.

The Daily Grill Studio City didn't fare so well; it was demolished. The ceiling caved in and the fire sprinklers went off and flooded the restaurant. Mother Nature acts without logic.

Our restaurant faced north and was ruined. The businesses in the same center that faced west did not have any damage at all.

I was scared. We didn't have earthquake insurance. The restaurant company was still small, and a total loss could have bankrupted us. Thanks to our insurance agent, Tim Milaney, we had fire sprinkler leakage coverage so that when the fire sprinklers went off and flooded the restaurant, all the damage was covered. Our business interruption insurance paid for the loss of business during the time it took to rebuild the restaurant. Having the appropriate insurance coverage saved my business career.

It took about three months to rebuild the restaurant. Then we had to go through the same process as opening a new restaurant. We couldn't expect our hourly team members to wait three months and they found other jobs. Some were so scared of another earthquake they moved out of California. We did the same pre-opening training meals and opened again. The opening was as busy as our original opening. Between the insurance which paid for the preopening expense as well as rebuilding the restaurant and the loyalty of the neighborhood, we were just as successful after the earthquake as before.

From that point on, Tim was the insurance agent for all our locations, and I helped him cover other restaurants as well. I was very loyal to him, and he truly appreciated it. His company still insures all our restaurants.

In 1995 we did a research study on what demographics our best Daily Grills had in common. The number one factor was that we had locations in business districts with numerous office buildings as well as residential surroundings with household incomes over $100,000. It was also important to have a variety of housing units nearby, like apartments or condominiums. We had seven restaurants in Southern California, and we knew that if we were to be considered more than a regional concept, we needed to open in a new city and state.

Chapter 15
Go East!

Our research pointed to Washington, D.C. as the area that had demographics most like Southern California, so we started looking for locations for a new Daily Grill. Leslie, Mike Weinstock, and I took about 10 trips in six months to scout locations. Since this was a new region, we knew we wouldn't get the kind of deals we were used to getting in Los Angeles. However, we felt if our first location in a major city was highly visible, that one good location could open the market for us.

There were many challenges in opening in another city, especially one that was 2,640 miles away. Even though we had a process in place, it was almost like opening our first restaurant. It was unfamiliar territory, but our past successes and research convinced us we were on the right track.

We had to make new contacts with service providers. We needed marketing to make sure people understood who we were and what we did. However, the biggest challenge was site selection.

We found a defunct men's clothing store at the northwest corner of 18th and M streets that looked like the best possible location. But there were a couple of problems. First of all, the location was a dry goods store, which meant it didn't have a restaurant exhaust system. Second, I had to convince the landlord's representative, a tough older man named Walter Cook, that a high-quality restaurant would be good for the building.

The building was owned by a wealthy widow, Mrs. Ring, whose husband left express instructions to protect it so it could be handed down to their daughter. I persuaded Walter to convince Mrs. Ring that we would be an asset to the building. I gave him the names of five of our landlords in Los Angeles who were very fond of me and whose property we had improved. They convinced Walter, who then convinced Mrs. Ring and her daughter, that a Daily Grill restaurant would enhance their building.

Next, I had to convince the city that they needed another restaurant in the area. We were within walking distance from the Dupont Circle Metro stop, and Metro stops were good locations for restaurants. The rent was the highest we ever paid of any location we had opened to date. Therefore, I had to convince our Board of Directors that expanding to Washington,

D.C. was a good move for the company. My credibility with the success of our other eight restaurants helped and they approved. I needed Board approval to spend the money to open the restaurant—no matter what city.

Mike Weinstock, one of the original partners, oversaw all construction and design and was there at least once a month. Chef John Sola moved to D.C. for six months to supervise the construction of the kitchen, hire and train the kitchen team members, and locate purveyors with the highest quality products. Once we opened, he worked side-by-side with the kitchen team, showing them how to prepare the food and place it on the plate, etc.

Leslie and I visited the location every few weeks while the restaurant was being built. Between all the travel and the cost of construction, this project was rapidly becoming a money pit and I knew this restaurant needed to be our most successful. Further expansion to D.C. and other cities hinged on it.

Six weeks prior to opening, we started hiring the team. This took about two weeks. Bill Shriver was our General Manager. Bill was originally from Baltimore, about 50 miles north of D.C.

He had moved to Los Angeles with his 5-year-old son Willie in 1992 and was General Manager of the Daily Grill in Studio City. We moved Bill back to Baltimore to run the Washington D.C. Daily Grill.

When Leslie and I came back to D.C. just before construction started, Bill informed me that we needed a larger bar. It seems the people in D.C. drink a lot more than in Los Angeles. It was a good thing I listened to Bill, for he was right, and we redesigned the restaurant to have about 25% of the dining room dedicated to the bar. The restaurant was built, and it was time to train the new team.

Thanks to Chuck Frank's business knowledge, we had training manuals and job descriptions for every position. We also had a training team of four servers, one bartender, four cooks, and three managers that came in from Los Angeles.

As was our tradition, before opening to the public we held "Training Meals." We invited about 50 people for lunch and dinner on the first of three nights. The second day we invited 100 people for lunch and dinner and the third day we invited 150 people for each meal.

The guest list for the D.C. training meals was comprised of the members of the Special Olympics committee. Bill Shriver, our general manager, was second cousin to Sargent Shriver, brother-in-law to John F. Kennedy. Eunice Shriver (John F. Kennedy's sister) started the Special Olympics and her husband Sargent served as its president. The proceeds of the training meals were donated to the Special Olympics.

This time, we also decided to open for Sunday brunch and invited 100 people for the Sunday brunch training. The brunch invitation list included parishioners from the nearby Saint Mary, Mother of God Catholic Church.

The week before the training meals were scheduled to start, Chef John Sola let me know he would not be ready for the Sunday Brunch training meal, which was the first of the training meals. So, we skipped the first Sunday and rescheduled the Sunday Brunch training meal to the following Sunday; we would do the other meals first.

Emails and letters were sent to everyone who had made Sunday Brunch reservations to let them know the meal was being pushed back one week. Everybody rescheduled for the following Sunday, except for one man who didn't get the message. He came to the door that first Sunday. I was there, apologized to him, and invited him to come the following Sunday. He was so upset he told me he would not come the following week and that he would NEVER come to the restaurant. He then sent me a letter expressing his displeasure about the change in the schedule and went on to tell me we would fail at the location and further predicted that we wouldn't even last one year. I responded with a letter of my own inviting him and three guests to come to the restaurant any day after we were open, and I would buy all of their meals. He sent my letter back, refused my offer, and reiterated that he would never come into the restaurant.

We opened in 1996 and it was a banner year. The Washington, D.C. Daily Grill was the busiest of all our restaurants, including The Grill on the Alley in Beverly Hills. Bill really saved us with his idea to enlarge the bar as it came to represent 24% of total sales; the restaurants in Los Angeles were under 10% in alcohol sales. This restaurant was not only the busiest one we ever had, it was the busiest restaurant and bar in the entire Washington, D.C. metro area and became the "go to" place for politicians. On any given day you could see a member of the President's cabinet, a senator, or any number of Congress members dining at the Daily Grill, which was voted the "best new restaurant" in Washington D.C. by one of the city's monthly magazines.

On the one-year anniversary of the D.C. Daily Grill, I thought I'd try again to get the man who missed the Sunday Brunch to come in. I sent another letter letting him know we had made our first year and invited him and three friends for dinner on me. He sent the letter back, again refusing my offer. I sent him a final letter stating that while I was not Catholic, I knew that a principle of Catholicism was forgiveness, and I was asking for his forgiveness in not communicating the training brunch meal rescheduling. I never heard from him. And here it is, 25 years later, and we are still in Washington, D.C.

Sometime in 1998 my old friend Larry Shupnick contacted me. He worked for a hotel company that owned the Georgetown Inn, a boutique hotel in Georgetown. We made a deal for the hotel to license the Daily Grill and contract us, Grill Concepts, Inc., to run the restaurant. This was a new deal structure for us and allowed us to open another restaurant in Washington, D.C. without putting any of GCI's capital into the deal.

This restaurant really surprised us. The lunch and dinner business attracted the D.C. lawyers and politicians. Former Secretary of State Madeleine Albright was a regular customer at the Georgetown Inn. When she was in town, she came into the restaurant three days a week. Secretary Albright always sat in the dining room, as far from the noise of the bar as possible.

The bar business was even bigger than the dining service; due in large part to the proximity of Georgetown University. It was wall-to-wall business seven nights a week from 8 p.m. to 2 a.m. Personally, I never wanted to run a bar and this experience validated my concerns. The clientele consisted of university students and young professionals who lived and worked in the area. With a hundred or so people jamming into the relatively small bar every night and drinking all night long, there was bound to be problems. Fortunately, whenever an altercation broke out, the security personnel would contain the problem before it escalated into something more serious. We had a doorman whose only job was to check I.D.'s. We also had two security people on all night. This lasted for about six or seven years until the next "big thing" opened and the clientele moved from our bar to the new one. Running this restaurant was not like any other restaurant we ever had before or after, and proved to me that I was not cut out for running bars.

If we hadn't moved to Washington, D.C. or another region of the U.S., we would not have been able to grow the way we did. Now we had two high-volume, high-visibility restaurants which made making real estate deals in the D.C. area a lot easier than when we first entered the market. It gave us a more level playing field like we had in Los Angeles. By that, I mean that the landlords we approached realized that having a Daily Grill in their region was a good draw for business.

Our next Daily Grill was in Tysons Corner Center, a major regional mall in Virginia, which was considered part of the Washington, D.C. metropolitan area. We were getting good Tenant Improvement allowances in the top malls in the area. There were two Tysons Corner regional malls; the one we went into was newer and not as well-known or visited. This was something that we, as outsiders, didn't realize. We also had a location on the second floor which didn't get a lot of traffic, but this was a familiar situation. We'd run into a similar circumstance with the Newport Beach Fashion Island mall restaurant. The Tysons Corner Regional Mall was also one of our biggest restaurants, seating 250 people.

Despite the seating capability, this restaurant was never able to fill to capacity, making it one of our least profitable restaurants. However, it taught me that you tend to spend more time in the restaurants that are less successful than you do in the restaurants that were most successful. You are always trying to figure out how to make the less successful restaurants busier.

We stayed in the location, profitably, for 10 years and when the lease was up, we decided not to renew. After this experience, we were much more careful about going into second story locations. They worked much better in the smaller "strip" malls than in the regional malls.

We opened the fourth east coast Daily Grill in Bethesda, Maryland, just northwest of the D.C. metropolitan area in 1999. This restaurant was part of the Hyatt Regency Bethesda, which was quite old and very busy. The hotel was on Wisconsin Avenue, one of the most heavily traveled highways from Maryland to Washington, D.C., and near a busy metro station known as Bethesda Metro Center. As this restaurant was in a hotel, it served three meals a day, and was quite lively. We drew clientele from the business community, hotel guests, and commuters dropping by for Happy Hour, all which made this location an above-average performer.

We worked hard on our local marketing due to the face it was considered a "hotel restaurant" and we were set back about 100 yards from Wisconsin Boulevard. We had a grand opening for this restaurant, which was not something we normally did. It was a very large event featuring Maryland Blue Crabs, which were a big deal in Maryland. We bought 500 pounds of the crabs and had a special introductory price. In 1999, Blue Crab dinners sold for about $30 a person for dinner. We were selling them for $10.

Bill Shriver and I thought this would be a BIG deal - but it wasn't. We had a whole refrigerated truck full of Blue Crabs and only about three days to sell them. After two days I could see I had to get rid of 300 pounds of crabs. I called a local seafood purveyor and sold them for $1 a pound. We lost $9 a pound. I never did that again. Even though our Grand Opening was a flop, the restaurant became a good performer.

With four Daily Grill restaurants in the Washington, D.C. market and seven Daily Grills in Southern California, it was time to explore additional avenues for growth. Our brand was well known, and we needed to find a way to leverage it.

The next phase of our development was to open Daily Grills in hotels across the U.S. Lew Wolff, a serious investor in GCI and a successful businessman, owned several hotels across the

U.S. Back in 1988, Lew flew me out to San Jose to his five-star San Jose Fairmont Hotel located in the heart of Silicon Valley, and convinced me this was the right place for The Grill on the Alley to have another restaurant. In those days, we needed to do at least $3 million in sales to make it work and I doubted that could happen. I told Lew I didn't think it was a good location for The Grill. He asked me how much business we needed to do to make it a successful restaurant. I told him, he thought for a minute and said, "Here is the deal." He offered a percentage- only lease. They wouldn't charge rent on the first $3 million in sales and we would only start paying 10 percent as rent on sales between $3 million and $4 million. All sales over $4 million would be charged at 15 percent. The Grill did $4 million in sales the first year at the Fairmont. This is when Lew came up with the idea of having Daily Grills replace the generic restaurants in his and other hotels.

We first tested the concept in a Hilton Hotel he owned in Burbank, which was directly across the street from the Hollywood Burbank airport. The deal structure went this way: the hotel owner would own the restaurant; GCI would be contracted to operate the restaurant and we would split the profit. GCI would get a six percent management fee before the profit split. The hotel paid all the costs to remodel the space and open the restaurant to Daily Grill specifications. As GCI was in charge of operations, we were assured the restaurant lived up to our standards.

The Daily Grill more than doubled the sales volume of the generic hotel restaurant. It was truly a win-win. Daily Grill restaurants were built without using our corporate funds and the hotels got a restaurant that improved the guest experience for the hotel. The hotel guests were unaware the restaurant and the hotel were not one business.

Lew decided this could be a good business for his son, Keith. We became partners and Keith went out and sold the concept to other hotels. Over the next five years, we opened Daily Grills in Hilton Hotels in Burbank, CA and Salt Lake City, Utah; Westin hotels in Portland, OR and Houston, TX; the Handlery Hotel in San Francisco, the Sheraton in Seattle, WA, and the Hyatt Regency in Tulsa, OK. This worked so well we also opened The Grill on the Alley's in the Westin hotel in Chicago, IL in addition to the Fairmont Hotel in San Jose.

In 1996 I was contacted by Jon Luther from CA One, an airport restaurant company. Jon wanted to know if the Daily Grill would be a part of their bid to open restaurants at the Los Angeles International Airport (LAX). I certainly was interested.

The first thing I thought of was my father. He lived in LA long before there was an airport. I knew if he were alive, he would be very proud and excited at the proposition of his son opening a restaurant at LAX. Jon went on to tell me his idea was to have two of Los Angeles' iconic restaurants as part of their bid. The other restaurant he was interested in was Wolfgang Puck Cafe.

This was at a time when most of the food concepts at airports across America were McDonalds, Kentucky Fried Chicken, and other fast-food franchises. Jon's idea was to bring the most popular restaurants in the city to that city's airports. He was the visionary of the concept which is now found in all major airports across America and in Europe as well.

CA One won the bid and built a Daily Grill at the Bradley International Terminal at LAX. The Daily Grill restaurant opened in January 1997 and, at the time, was considered the most forward-thinking restaurant in any airport in the country.

Not only did we get the Daily Grill in the airport, Jon and his wife Sharon became life-long friends with Leslie and me. Jon went on to be the President of Popeye's Chicken and later became the Chairman & CEO of Dunkin' Brands, the owners of Dunkin' Donuts and Baskin-Robbins Ice Cream.

Vice President Joe Biden outside the Daily Grill, Washington D.C.

Chapter 16
Commencement

In early 2000, I was asked by the Dean of Collins College, Bob Small, to give the commencement address at Cal Poly Pomona University.

At that time, I had been on the Board of Advisors for Collins College for about 15 years, had donated money, and also served as president of the Education Foundation. As I grew into adulthood, education was now something I valued, which was contradictory to my early school years of just trying to get by. Even so, I was stunned. I barely made it through high school and, truth be told, was ashamed that I had never been to college. How could they possibly want *me* to give the commencement address?

But they did and so I swallowed my misgivings and got to work.

Standing on the stage, dressed in a cap and gown for the first time in my life, I looked at the eager, young faces of these new graduates and spoke about how important it was to NEVER give up. I told them the *whole* story of my learning disabilities, how they affected me throughout my life, and the problems I had growing up and in my 20s and 30s. I told them that integrity, tenacity, and hard work was my road to success. When I finished, the students gave me a standing ovation.

When I was leaving the stage, Bob Suzuki, the president of the University, came up to me. He thanked me for all I had given the school and for the honesty and integrity I gave to the students. But the most inspiring thing he said to me was how sorry he was that his teenaged son wasn't there to hear me. He went on to tell me about his son's learning disabilities and that he would have been inspired to hear my commencement address. He later got a video tape of my address and played it for his son and then called to let me know how much his son appreciated hearing my story.

Since that address some 20 years ago, I have had at least 10 of the graduating students contact me to let me know how inspirational my commencement address was to them. They realized the importance of their education that they didn't fully realize when they were in school; that it wasn't necessarily *what* they learned but that they *learned* how to learn.

In all my years of volunteering and working with organizations, this experience returned something more meaningful than all the time and money I had ever given; it raised my self-esteem to an amount that couldn't be calculated. Even though I had become successful in business, I always felt I was "lacking" because I didn't go to college and these feelings of somehow being "less than" followed me all my life. Standing on that stage and sharing my story with these bright, young graduates on the threshold of their lives felt like a personal commencement for me.

When you are asked to donate or volunteer your time, say yes. Helping others is good for your soul.

Chapter 17
Forming Spivak & Frank

In 2005 I was 62 years old, operating 25 restaurants, running a company with over $100M in sales, and spending most of my time as an administrator, not an operator. I felt the company might be better off having someone with corporate restaurant experience.

I contacted Philip Gay, the former CFO at California Pizza Kitchen. After CPK sold to PepsiCo, Inc., Philip left the company and moved to Texas where he ran a candy company. I asked Philip if he was interested in moving his family back to Los Angeles and becoming our CFO with the understanding that when I retired, he would then become the CEO of Grill Concepts, Inc. Philip was quite interested and came to work with us.

After about six months, I knew Philip was my choice to replace me and I was ready to make the move. We worked out a six-month plan where I would train Philip. During that time, we visited all 25 of our restaurants and made the announcement that I was retiring and Philip would become the new CEO. Six months later, in January 2006, I retired and Philip became President and CEO and Mike Weinstock and I became co-chairs of GCI.

Just at that time, I was contacted by Kevin Boylan and T.K. Pillan. Both men were strict Vegans and wanted to open a total plant-based restaurant. I tried, desperately, to talk them out of it because in 2006, I didn't think there were enough vegans to support this concept—vegan isn't the same as vegetarian—but they were adamant and so I agreed to help them.

I suggested they consider it a plant-based concept as the

word "vegan" could be misconstrued as something with more of a cult following at the time. I consulted with them on every aspect of opening a restaurant with expectations of developing a chain of restaurants.

Leslie and I took Kevin to the National Restaurant Association Show in Chicago where we found several plant-based proteins suppliers and computer systems. They hired an accomplished vegan chef named Ray White, who became a co-owner. I worked with Ray to line up plant-based purveyors and recruit cooks. I even suggested the name Veggie Grill. They opened the first Veggie Grill in Irvine, California in 2006. I then took a seat on their Board of Directors and stayed until 2008. They currently have 29 restaurants in four states.

During this time, I called Chuck Frank, the consultant I had hired several years ago to help consolidate the restaurant businesses, to tell him I was leaving GCI and was ready to form the consulting company we had always talked about. As Chuck came from the accounting side of the business and I was from operations, we felt we had a compelling story to tell other people interested in opening restaurants or help existing restaurant companies. We formed a company called Spivak & Frank Restaurant Development. *Nation's Restaurant News* wrote a story about us and right away, we had several calls, including one from my friend Jon Luther, then President and CEO of Dunkin' Brands, the parent company of Dunkin' Donuts and Baskin-Robbins.

For Dunkin' Donuts to be successful they needed their customers to have Dunkin' be their choice for coffee. As Jon put it: "People eat donuts one or two times a week while they drink coffee every day. Sometimes two or three times a day." Jon hired us to design a new concept for Dunkin' Donuts; an "experience" store to help change consumer perception by demonstrating Dunkin's coffee credentials and to serve as an example for opening stores in new territories.

The new experience store comprised three distinct areas: a coffee department complete with a coffee expert, a traditional donut store, and a children's area where parents could leave their kids while they shopped. Unfortunately, it remained a concept. Jon retired and the person who followed him didn't implement the experience store. But, Dunkin' Donuts did expand their brand awareness and is now well-known for their coffee.

Next, we were contacted by a young man named Brent Stein who had an MBA from the University of California Berkeley. He had an idea to have a quick, casual restaurant concept selling bao, which were steamed buns normally found at Chinese restaurants. They would cut open the bao bun and fill it with several Asian-flavored proteins in sauce, much like a small Taco. The concept would be called Take A Bao.

We opened the first restaurant in the dining hall at the Westfield Mall in Century City, a suburb of Los Angeles. We opened a second, free-standing location in Studio City, a Los Angeles suburb in the San Fernando Valley. After the opening of the second store, Brent didn't need us anymore and went out on his own. Our job was to help get the door open, and that was done. He ran both locations for several years and then decided to leave the restaurant business.

Then Jon Luther called again— this time to design a new concept for Baskin-Robbins which needed a new, more modern store to showcase its 31 flavors of ice cream. After they opened in a mall on the property of the New England Patriots football stadium in Foxborough, Massachusetts, they franchised and used it as a model for new stores. By this time, the recession of 2007 and 2008 had taken its toll on GCI. It seems the company had expanded too fast and got into financial trouble.

Enter Chuck Mathewson who purchased more stock to bail the company out of financial trouble and became the major stockholder of GCI. Toward the end of 2008, Chuck Mathewson called to set up a meeting with me. He asked if I would come back and run the company again. I told him I would do it for three years and train someone to replace me. I then called my partner, Chuck Frank, and let him know I would no longer be able to work with him at Spivak & Frank. Chuck formed his own company, and I went back to work at GCI. After about two years, GCI was back on solid footing. By that time, I wanted to open a new concept which would appeal to a younger demographic.

Chapter 18
Public School

My son, Jason, worked for Sony Pictures and was transferred to London in the early 2000s. Leslie and I visited Jason and his wife, Laurie, several times and each time, they would take us to a gastropub for dinner. While we were familiar with the traditional English pub, these gastropubs were something new to us.

The concept was started by classic-trained British chefs who, wanting to open their own restaurants with minimal capital, bought old pubs with small kitchens. Pubs typically focused on beer sales and if they did serve food, it was traditional dishes like Shepherd's Pie or Ploughman's Lunch (a cold meal of bread, meat, and cheese). These chefs had a different vision for their small pubs: they would serve quality food along with a range of craft beers and the gastropub was born.

These trips to London weren't like the other times when Leslie and I traveled to research restaurants. I wasn't looking to start a new business, I just wanted to spend time with my son and his wife. But after several visits to various gastropubs, I wanted to open one in California. The gastropub was a youthful concept that would appeal to and attract a younger demographic than our other restaurants. The Grill on the Alley attracted the 50+ age group and the Daily Grill appealed to the 40 to 60+ age groups. We believed the 20 to 40-year-olds would embrace the gastropub concept.

The craft beer movement hadn't yet gained momentum in the United States. People weren't really savvy about beer. A Heineken beer was considered exotic beyond the usual

Budweiser or Miller Lite. And, like years ago before people realized there was more to wine than just "red" or "white," I felt consumers could be educated about craft beers. I was ready to take a chance.

The 2008 recession affected all our restaurants but the downtown Los Angeles location really took a hit. Even four years later, many of the office buildings which had been full before the recession were still barely half-full. I thought we could stimulate the area by opening a gastropub in the bar of the downtown Los Angeles Daily Grill. It would be two restaurants in one: when you came through the front door, the Daily Grill would be to the left and the gastropub to the right. Leveraging the space and resources of a restaurant we already owned was a good way to test the concept.

I called my financial partner, Chuck Mathewson, and told him my idea. When he asked how much money we would need I said about $500,000. His answer was, "I'd rather try it and fail than not try it at all. Where do I send the check?"

Now we had to develop the concept. I met with our executive team and explained what we were going to do. Chef John Sola and Phil Kastel, Vice President of Culinary, would design the gastropub menu. Phil designed new dishes to serve in all our restaurants. Thomas Kachani, Senior Vice President of Operations, along with Louie Feinstein, the Vice President of Operations were in charge of hiring, training dining personnel, and all functions having to do with dining room functions. Terri Henry, Vice President of Marketing, handled the marketing, menu design, merchandising, and logo application, and Mike Weinstock worked on the physical design for the pub.

We also needed a name for the pub and everyone had different ideas. I wanted the iBar. Terri suggested Public School. I liked it. Public schools were unpretentious,

173

democratic, and open to everyone.

Mike and I hired an architect named George Kelley and interior designer Jen Smith. We wanted the space to be of our own modern-day genre, not a carbon copy of an English pub. George and Jen created a classic bar and dining area with leather booths. Between the two of them and Mike directing the design, we ended up with a great mix of old pub and school implements like old Olivetti typewriters and small cooking utensils like wood mortar and pestle, cookie cutters, chocolate molds, and vintage scales.

Terri further developed the public-school theme. The menu was modeled after the black-and-white speckled composition books we all used in school. The cocktail napkins had ruled lines like the paper we learned to print on in grammar school. Happy Hour was called Recess. Our marketing tag line was *Education in The Art of Food and Beer*.

Public School Menu, composition book cover

The culinary team needed to come up with a menu of special food items not available at other restaurants. Many of the food items were eclectic; we drew from the familiar foods and added our own twist. The traditional appetizer of Buffalo Chicken Wings became Buffalo Cauliflower. We offered other appetizers like Bacon and Cheddar Tots. Our entrees included Bangers and Mash, along with pizzas cooked in a wood-burning pizza oven. We had a great Hamburger, Lamb Burger, and BBQ Bison Burger. For side dishes we offered Shaved Brussels & Kale Slaw, and Grilled Broccolini. Desserts included a classic Lemon Meringue Pie.

We hired a craft beer expert named Hallie Beaune of The Beer Chicks. She knew everything there was to know about craft beer, and the key to Public School was the beer. Hallie also gave us credibility. The craft beer industry was anti-chain and our company was exactly what the craft brewers *didn't* want to be. Hallie's reputation and relationships helped us gain credibility and introductions to the brew masters so they understood we were serious about the industry.

Public School – Culver City, CA

Public School opened in July 2010. At first, people thought it was a cooking school, but soon understood they were getting a choice of two restaurants in one location.

The gastropub featured small breweries that brewed only craft beers and we highlighted 32 beers at a time. When someone ordered a Budweiser, the bartender would tell them we only featured craft beers and then give small tastes of beers similar to what they had ordered. This worked well because if you liked the beer served at Public School, you had to come back. It would be hard to find another bar that had the same craft beer selection.

We also held Beer 101 classes where one of our brewery's Brew Masters would come and talk to our guests. The two-hour class cost $50 per person and included four different beers, each paired with a food dish. It was very educational and entertaining. The class was so popular it usually took about three weeks to get a spot.

We knew after six months that Public School was successful and thought that if we found a stand-alone location for another Public School, we could have another big hit like the Daily Grill.

We opened the first free-standing Public School in Culver City in 2011. We chose Culver City for several reasons. There were a lot of businesses and offices in the area. The main offices and sound studio for Sony Pictures as well as several other smaller motion picture companies were within walking distance to our location.

The day we opened, people waited in line on the sidewalk for a table. The wait for dinner was sometimes 1 ½ hours. We would take their names then call their cell phone and let them know their table would be ready in 5 to 7 minutes. As the former Chairperson of the California Restaurant Association, with its over 20,000 members, I knew what kind of sales-per-seat the highest volume restaurants in the state did and we ranked better than all of them. Sales-per-seat is one of the best metrics for judging the success of a restaurant.

Based on the success of the Culver City Public School, we opened the second standalone gastropub in the back of the Promenade at Westlake, a successful luxury shopping center. Our location in the mall was next to The Grill on the Alley. Despite the fact our restaurant was in a Caruso-built mall, which are known across the U.S. and very successful, this Public School was in the very back of the mall and hard to find.

Public School restaurant, Culver City, CA

Now, you'd think I would have learned from prior experience with the Daily Grills and mall locations, but I'm afraid my ego took over. I felt the Public School was such a great draw and that if you did the right thing and did it well, provided value, great food and entertainment, people would find you. This had been the case with the Grill on the Alley but The Grill had a check spending average of $70 per person and the Public School customer's average spend was $25 per person; the location wasn't strong enough to get three times the number of people to come in and meet a similar per-person sales target. The Westlake Public School sales were more than enough to make a profit but the restaurant just didn't perform the way we hoped it would.

A year later we opened a Public School on the corner of Sepulveda and Ventura boulevards in Sherman Oaks. This location was our highest volume Pubic School restaurant. This locale had everything we needed: a business community strong enough to deliver a week-day lunch trade and residential demographics to support dinner seven nights a week. Sepulveda and Ventura was the third busiest intersection in Los Angeles and surrounded by office buildings and a high-income, high density, residential neighborhood and a mall across the street with a movie theatre. We were lucky to find this location. This gastropub even had a game room where the guests played Beer Pong, darts, and Jenga, which were popular with the younger crowd.

Based on these successes, we went on to open Public School gastropubs in Summerlin, a suburb of Las Vegas, Denver, two in Dallas, and one in Atlanta, following the same opening processes as we did for the Daily Grills.

Four years after the first Public School opened inside the Daily Grill, we now had eight gastropubs in four states. The craft beer industry has flourished in the U.S. Brew pubs are no longer a curiosity. We didn't start the trend, but we like to think we helped it along and provided our guests with an *Education in The Art of Food and Beer.*

Chapter 19
Life with Leslie

That long-ago luncheon at the Bel-Air Sands Hotel in Brentwood not only brought me new business opportunities but more importantly, an unexpected opportunity to find everlasting love in the chance reunion with Leslie. We have had many adventures over the years and I like to think that's one of the reasons she finally agreed to marry me.

Bob and Leslie Spivak at The Grill on the Alley, New Year's Eve, 2010

Birthday Surprise

February 26, 1983 was Leslie's 40th birthday and I planned a surprise. At that time, we had been together one year. I invited her to the apartment I shared with my roommate, Allan, and told her I was going to cook dinner for her birthday.

What Leslie didn't know was that I had also invited all the friends we had in common, including my father. Twenty people yelled "Surprise!" when she opened the door. This was the start of a 40-year tradition of surprising Leslie on her birthday.

Some of the birthday "surprises" consisted of a special night out and others were trips ranging from two nights to a week. For the overnight trips I would tell her what to pack but not where we were going or what we were going to do. Some people don't like surprises but thankfully, Leslie always went along with my plans and embraced the adventure.

For her 50th birthday, I told her to pack like we were going to stay at a golf resort in Phoenix. We drove to the airport, flew to San Francisco, and then sat in the terminal at the gate of the plane going to Phoenix. But my eyes were focused on the nearby gate – the real gate. When Leslie got up to go to the bathroom, I went over to let the gate agent know I was surprising my wife and we would be the last to board. When our plane was fully boarded, I said, "Let's go!" and quickly led her to the ramp to board our plane, all without her seeing the airplane's true destination.

When we were seated, I had to make a decision. I knew the pilot was going to come on the speaker and announce the destination and I could have diverted her attention and kept her in suspense but I didn't think it was fair to keep her in suspense for the entire five-hour flight so we listened to the pilot's announcement. When Leslie heard our destination, she let out a yell of surprise—we were going to Maui!

We stayed at the Four Seasons Hotel and after unpacking, sat on the balcony overlooking the Pacific Ocean where I brought out another surprise. Letters. I had asked her sister and friends to write how they felt about Leslie on her 50th birthday. We opened a bottle of Champagne I had brought along and started reading the letters. The touching words from family friends had us both in tears.

We have had 41 wonderful years together, each year capped

off with a birthday surprise, and they're just going to keep on coming.

Our Wedding

Leslie and I lived together for 11 years before we got married. Everyone thought I was the one that didn't want to get married, but this couldn't be further from the truth. Every year I asked Leslie to marry me and every year she would say the same thing: "We are so happy together and I don't want it to change."

Finally, after 11 years, I promised her that if we got married it would never change, and she said yes! I wanted to have a wedding and she just wanted to get married. I proposed just having a party and when everyone got there, we'd get married. In effect, this would be a surprise wedding, but the surprise would be on our guests. She liked the idea and that is just what we did.

We planned for the date of July 10th which was 10 days after my 50th birthday. We met with Rabbi David Baron to explain what we were going to do. He was a little nervous as he had never presided over a surprise wedding. He was sworn to secrecy; he couldn't tell anyone. The guest list included about 150 people who were told they were invited to a summer party at our house. The only people who really knew what we were up to were Leslie's father and our four children.

To seat that many people we had to cover our pool and hot tub with scaffolding which became a stage for us to make the announcement. The Grill on the Alley catered the party. We hired valets to park all the cars, a five-piece band, and a dance floor. My friend Helen Bernstein was going to be in Washington, D.C., at that time. Now, Helen was the friend I had called in the early morning hours so many years ago after Leslie and I had spent all night talking. I told Helen, without letting her know the reason, how important it was to me for her to be here. Being the dear friend she was, Helen flew home two days early so she could attend the party.

When all our guests had arrived, I stood on the makeshift platform and made the following announcement. "There has been a lot of talk about the reason for this party. Some people thought we were going to announce our engagement, which I told them was not true. Someone even thought we had gotten married, and that was what we were going to announce. I told them NO we didn't get married. Most people thought it was for my 50th birthday. Most of you know me well enough to know I wouldn't do an elaborate party like this one for *my* birthday. But there is a reason for this party. Our Rabbi is here, and you have not come to a party, you have come to a wedding and the ceremony is NOW!"

Everyone started yelling and clapping. The Grill team came running out from the kitchen yelling, "they are getting married!" I told everyone that Leslie was going to change her clothes and the ceremony would start in 15 minutes.

Leslie's father, Syd, walked her out. Our four children each held one pole of the Chuppah (canopy) and the Rabbi got ready. We faced the Rabbi with our backs to our guests. Just before he started, Leslie said, "Wait a minute."

I thought she was going to call the whole thing off. Instead, she said to the Rabbi, "We want to face our friends." The Rabbi traded places with us so we could face our guests.

The ceremony commenced, and we were married! Everyone was so excited and today, people still talk about it. Michael Jackson (not the singer), who had a talk radio program on KABC at the time, talked about the wedding on the air the following Monday. When asked why we did a surprise wedding, we answered, "We have too many toasters." We didn't want wedding presents, we just wanted to share the event with our friends and family.

Knife Meets Finger: A Turkish Cooking Class

When Leslie and I travel we always try and take a cooking class in the country we visit. Several years ago, we were in Istanbul, Turkey and had reserved a cooking class through Trip Advisor. We had trouble finding out where the class was being taught. Turns out the class was being held in a woman's apartment on the sixth floor of a building which had no elevator. By the time we found the address and walked up the six flights of stairs, we were about 10 minutes late.

When we walked into the cooking teacher's living room, she and three other couples were waiting for us. By the way she glared at us, I could tell she was annoyed that we were late. She went on, in a very stern way, to tell us the rules of the class: we must all wear aprons when cooking, the women had to tie their hair back off their face, and no one was allowed to use their utensils until she told us to. She was a very large woman and you could tell she was used to giving orders. I almost felt like I was on the first day of a new cooking job.

Just about the time she had finished telling us the rules, her little dog trotted into the room with a bra and panties hanging in his mouth. She was so embarrassed she grabbed the undergarments from the dog and ran into her bedroom. When she came out, she was a different person and quietly said, "Let's go into the kitchen and start cooking."

The first recipe we were going to make was Turkish Moussaka, a delicious eggplant dish. The instructor had very bad knife skills. As she was cutting the eggplant, the knife sliced her finger. I knew from my restaurant cooking days just what to do in this situation. I grabbed a towel and wrapped it tightly around her finger, like a tourniquet. I then told her to hold her hand high over her head to keep the blood from rushing to the cut. Then I took over the class. We used her recipes and cooked the entire meal. Each time she dropped her hand below her waist, I told her to hold it up. Those were *my* rules.

The food was great, and afterward, everyone thanked me for finishing the class—without having to listen to her long list of rules. I'm sure that after everyone left, she had to go to the emergency hospital and get her finger stitched up.

Champagne and History – A Perfect Blend

In October 1987, after The Grill had been open for two years, Leslie and I traveled to France with a group of ten restaurateurs and their wives. We all met at the Hotel De Crillon in Paris where we boarded a bus and started our odyssey. The first stop was in a little town named Chablis in North Central France, where Chablis wine is made. We were the guests of Christian Moreau, the great-great grandson of Joseph Moreau who founded the winery in 1814. Christian gave us a grand tour and tasting and put us all up at the Hotel du Vieux Moulin.

The second day we drove to Burgundy and were guests of The Confrerie des Chevailers du Tastevin which is a society dedicated to promoting all things Burgundian, especially Burgundy wines. The two main grape varietals in Burgundy are Pinot Noir and Chardonnay.

The highlight of the Burgundy tour was Domaine de la Romanee-Conti. Romanee-Conti wines are the most famous and expensive wines of Burgundy. In 1945, Romanee-Conti broke the record for the two most expensive bottles of wine selling for $558,000 and $496,000. Currently, the wine sells for an average of $20,000 a bottle. The most interesting fact about the vineyard is it's only 4.47 acres, which is very small compared to vineyards in Napa Valley which are well over 100 acres. Whereas most vineyards are owned by investment groups, Romanee-Conti has a total of eight investors that each own their own row or two of the most expensive wine grapes in the world. Normally, investors would own a percentage of the winery, not the vines. The winery produces about 6,000 bottles a year. Almost all the wine is contracted for by wine collectors and three-star Michelin restaurants and it is almost impossible to buy the wine. While we got the tour, they didn't give us a wine tasting.

Champagne was the final wine region we visited. There are three major towns in Champagne: Reims, Epernay, and Troyes. Sparkling Wine can be made all over the world but to call it Champagne, it must be made in the Champagne region of France. The two main wine varietals grown and used in making Champagne are Chardonnay and Pinot Noir.

Our group was entertained by all ten of these Champagne houses. Their wines are stored in underground caves carved out of chalk, which is what makes their Champagne so special. The underground chalk caves maintain a constant temperature of 53 degrees all year around and the chalk walls soak up moisture, keeping the humidity at a consistent 88 percent; all perfect conditions for storing Champagne.

The most exciting day we had on the trip was a lunch in the caves of La Maison Mumm's champagne house. While we were all in the cave getting ready for a beautiful five-course lunch, an Oompah band came in to serenade us. The band members were men, all well into their 60s. After playing three songs, one of the older men spoke about why they wanted to come into the cave and play for us.

During the second world war, the French hid the town's Jewish citizens in the caves. They were later liberated by the Americans in November 1944. *The members of the band, now playing their music for this group of Americans in the chalk caves, were amongst those that had been freed from these very caves by American soldiers.*

At this point we were all in tears. This was truly one of the most touching and memorable experiences of my life.

The tour was over and we drove back to Paris. I told Hal Rosoff, the leader of the group, the story about L'Ami Louis, the restaurant I had read about in Mimi Sheraton's article which became the inspiration for The Grill's oak-fired charcoal broiler. We all went there for dinner one night and when I walked through the doors, tears streamed down my cheeks. The restaurant looked just like I imagined: white walls, dark green upholstered leather booths, and an oak-fired broiler which could be seen from the dining room. When I read Mimi Sheraton's article all those years ago, I never, in my wildest dreams, expected to someday be having dinner in that restaurant. Just as I never expected to have my own restaurant.

Wrigley Field

Leslie and I were at the National Restaurant Association Show in Chicago in May 1989. I mentioned that I had never been to a Chicago Cubs baseball game at Wrigley Field, which was on my "Bucket List." Leslie said, "Why don't we go?"

I checked the schedule and saw there was a night game on Thursday, May 19th. We didn't have tickets, so we just decided to take the "L" (Chicago's Metro elevated train) to the stadium. We got there about 6:15 p.m. which was perfect since the game started at 7:10 p.m. I went to the ticked counter and asked for two tickets. I really didn't care where we sat, I just wanted to be at Wrigley Field. The man behind the counter told me all the seats were sold out and all that was available was "standing room only."

I had heard the expression but didn't realize it was a real thing. We bought two standing-room tickets. I asked a man outside the stadium if this was a special game because it was sold out. He looked at me like I was crazy and let me know this was the first year Wrigley Field had lights and that all the night games were sold out for the year. It seems since Wrigley Field opened in 1914, they only played day games until 1988.

Leslie and I went into the stadium and stood in the "standing-room only" area when the game started. After about three innings, it got very cold and we were not comfortable standing. I told her we could go, but I just wanted to go to the front of the stadium where the white façade with the iconic sign read "Welcome to Wrigley Field" in blinking lights that made it look like the words were "traveling" across the sign.

We walked to the front of the stadium and crossed the road to the intersection of Clark and Addison streets, where I wanted to take a picture. Just as I raised my camera, a Chicago policeman grabbed me by the arm and said in a very stern voice, "WHAT DO YOU THINK YOU'RE DOING?"

I was totally scared and sheepishly said, "I'm taking a picture."

"Not here you don't. Come with me," he directed.

I wasn't sure if I was under arrest or what. Leslie, on the other hand, saw a little twinkle in his eyes. At that moment, he took a whistle out from around his neck, blew it in loud blasts to stop traffic from coming into the intersection, and marched me out to the middle of the street. While we were standing there, he started the traffic so it flowed in both directions around us and then said, "*This* is where you take the picture!"

Just as I put the camera up to my eye, he said, "Not yet." He waited for the traveling lights to come around and when they read "Welcome to Wrigley Field" he shouted, "Now!" He again blew his whistle to stop traffic and marched me back to the sidewalk. Leslie heard another policeman tell someone that "Mac was at it again."

We continued on to a local bar for a beer and watched the rest of the game on television. That was one baseball game I will never forget.

Cannes Film Festival

In May 1994 the Beverly Hills City Council invited Leslie and me to attend the Cannes Film Festival in Cannes, France. Beverly Hills is the "sister city" to Cannes. We were very excited to attend the festival and of course, said YES! I had never been to the South of France and wanted to see it all. We scheduled a flight to Nice to start our journey and also planned a week for a driving tour of Northern Italy after the film festival.

We had two big suitcases. The Film Festival was "Black Tie" so we had to have dress clothes and the trip to Italy was casual travel clothing. After three days in Nice we checked out of the Bristol Hotel and I asked the Concierge to get us a cab to Cannes.

"You don't take a cab to Cannes," the Concierge said. "You take the train."

When I told Leslie what the Concierge said, she said, "We have too much luggage to take the train."

I went to the Bell Captain and asked him to get us a cab to Cannes. He replied, "You don't take a cab to Cannes, you take the train."

Again, Leslie said we had too much luggage we take the train. I went to the front of the hotel to get a cab and the doorman said, "You take a cab to the train station and take the train to Cannes." At this point, I told Leslie we were taking the train.

When we got to the train station, as luck would have it, our train was across the tracks which meant we had to go down a stairway, walk underneath the train tracks, and then take another set of stairs up to the platform. Our two big suitcases were definitely an issue. Knowing Leslie had wanted to take a cab, I took charge of the luggage and loaded the suitcases onto a three-wheeled cart and started bouncing it down the stairs. Halfway down, the front wheel spun around and slammed me into the banister, right into the small of my back. I wasn't about to tell Leslie it hurt; I just went on to the bottom of the stairs. Then I had to carry the two heavy bags up the stairs. When our train came, it was all we could do to pile the bags into the coupling car before the train took off for Cannes. Here we were, huddled in the coupling car because we had too much baggage to drag to a seat. We stood there the next 40 minutes as we passed through the cities: Monte-Carlo, Antibes, and Monaco, before finally arriving in Cannes.

We took a cab from the train station to the hotel, changed into our fancy clothes, and started walking to the Cannes cocktail party honoring the contingent from Beverly Hills. As we walked along the beach, past the topless sunbathers, an ocean breeze came up and caused me to sneeze, a sneeze that caused excruciating pain and dropped me to one knee. It seems when the cart threw me against the banister at the train station, I broke a rib which didn't separate until I sneezed. We spent the rest of that day in a French hospital where they took x-rays and confirmed I had a broken rib. They gave me some pain medication and sent me on my way. We missed the cocktail party but made it to the dinner – also honoring the Beverly Hills contingent, the mayor of Cannes, and dignitaries from the Film Festival. That year, Quentin Tarantino's film "Pulp Fiction" received the grand prize Palme d'Or.

After the three-day festival, we headed to Tuscany, Italy, the home of Chianti wine. The entire countryside was in bloom and the air was full of pollen which aggravated my allergies. The last thing you want to do with a broken rib is sneeze and there was so much pollen in the air, we left Tuscany early and spent the rest of the trip in Portofino by the ocean. For the whole rest of the trip, I was in terrible pain, but I never mentioned it.

To Leslie's credit, she never said what I'm sure she was thinking: *we should have taken a cab!*

The Emperor is Naked! Or: Who Made the Macaroni and Cheese?

Leslie and I have hosted Thanksgiving dinner at our house since 1998. We usually have between 30 to 40 people including our four children and their families, which alone totals 20 people, Leslie's sister and her family, and anybody else we know who didn't have a place to go on Thanksgiving.

I make three or four turkeys; one is smoked and the rest are roasted and stuffed with two different kinds of stuffing. I also make two of everything else including candied yams, mashed potatoes, fresh cranberries, and all the trimmings.

Several years ago, when one of our children married, we were told their new spouse "Didn't eat turkey" or just about everything else traditionally associated with the holiday feast. Their mother served Stouffer's Macaroni and Cheese at Thanksgiving.

I decided I would make my own macaroni and cheese to add to the table for the new addition to our family. When I told Leslie my idea, she informed me the only macaroni and cheese this person would eat was Stouffer's.

We bought enough Stouffer's Macaroni and Cheese to accommodate the number of guests we were having. I thawed it out, placed it all in a Pyrex baking dish and put it in the oven. Just before it was done baking, I turned on the broiler and gave it a nice brown crust. And so, macaroni and cheese was added to the other 20-plus food offerings on our Thanksgiving table.

Well, our guests all *raved* about the macaroni and cheese because they thought I had made it from scratch. It was never my intention to fool anyone about who made the dish, but they all gushed about it so much I didn't have the nerve to tell them it was Stouffer's. And every year thereafter, people would say, "I hope you are making that fabulous macaroni and cheese again!"

It reminded me of the Hans Christian Andersen tale of "The Emperor's New Clothes," where an emperor believes he is "wearing" new clothes and parades through the village naked, believing he is clothed in the finest cloths, only to have the illusion shattered when one little boy dares to speak the truth that the emperor is naked. People all thought that "if Bob made the macaroni and cheese, it must be the best!" No one would have believed it was Stouffer's!

I guess that by telling this story now, everyone will know my secret—and come Thanksgiving, I'll be able to sleep better knowing the truth is out there.

Chapter 20
All in the Family

People always talk to me about how successful I've been. I respond the same way: I agree I'm very successful but not in the way you may think. I feel my success stems from the kind of father I've been.

The restaurant business is hard on families, as evidenced by my parents' divorce. It requires your constant attention, all day, every day. My father always found time to attend my games and I learned from his example: no matter how busy I was I had to make quality time to spend with my own children. Even though the restaurant business was demanding, you couldn't let it take over your life. I was proud of my kids and made time to attend their events. Like my mother who budgeted money for the monthly bills, I learned to budget my time for the important things, and nothing is more important than your children.

I hope that when my children look back, they never feel that I wasn't there for them. Jason and Lis would come and have lunch at Soup 'n Such, and later to The Grill when I was there, but it wasn't because that was the only way they could see me; they enjoyed coming to the restaurants and were proud of them. Coaching both Jason and Elissa's baseball teams was also a wonderful way to spend more time with them when they were young. Being a parent is the most important job and I wanted to be there for them.

I'm very proud of Jason and Elissa, and also of Leslie's children, Todd and Dayna. All of our children are self-sufficient and "good" people.

When my children were born, I knew my job was to give them a good education and every opportunity to do whatever it was they wanted to do. If they had an opportunity go to college,

I wanted to make sure they had the qualifications and finances to do so. I wanted them to care about *all* people, no matter their color, gender, or other affiliations. If, after having the opportunity to do whatever it was they wanted to do, whether it was to be a trash collector or another profession, and they were good, happy adults, I would be happy. Growing up, neither Jason or Elissa ever worked in one of my restaurants; if they had wanted to that would have been fine but I never pushed and they never gravitated toward the business.

Top Row:

(From left to right): Sydney Weill (Granddaughter), Todd Weill (Son), Jeff Golenberg (Son-in-law), Jordan Golenberg (Grandson), Bob Spivak (Me), Leslie Spivak, Laurie Spivak (Daughter in-law), Jason Spivak (Son), Elissa Marshall (Daughter), Scott Marshall (Son-in law)

Middle Row:

Deanne Weill (Daughter in-law), Dayna Golenberg (Daughter), Alex Golenberg (Granddaughter), Sylvie Spivak (Granddaughter), Sam Marshall (Grandson), Ethan Marshall (Grandson),

Front:

Jack Weill (Grandson), Carly Golenberg (Granddaughter)

I feel I've achieved my goal as a parent to Jason and Elissa as well as being a role model for Todd and Dayna. Leslie and I are very proud of all our children, their accomplishments, and the families they've built. Every parent just wants their children to be happy.

Jason Spivak

Jason was born in December 1968. When he was 10, I had the great pleasure of coaching him on his Little League team. He played 2nd base and got along with all the kids—I was so proud of what a team player he was. I coached his team for three years and it was a great time for us to bond through a shared love of baseball.

Jason attended University High School, the public school in the neighborhood, and then college at UCLA When he graduated. in 1991, he told me he had been in school for 17 years and just wanted to get a job to pay his rent and be self-sufficient.

During that time, he met a wonderful young woman named Laurie Palmer who became a serious girlfriend. Jason had been working at a store for three years when I encouraged him to go to business school. I felt having a business degree would open many career opportunities for him. He took the GMAT (Graduate Management Admissions Test) and applied to Wharton School of Business at the University of Pennsylvania. He graduated from Wharton with his MBA in 1997. Even though this was my son's accomplishment, the fact that I didn't go to college hung like a shadow over my life, and so watching Jason graduate from this distinguished college overwhelmed my emotions—in a good way!

MGM Motion Pictures recruited Jason and he went to work in Santa Monica. Jason and Laurie were married in November 1998 at the Los Angeles Union Train Station and The Grill catered their wedding. A couple years later, MGM offered him a two-year position in London, England. Simultaneously, Laurie applied for and received a Fulbright Scholarship, one of the most prestigious scholarship programs in the world, to attend the London School of Economics where she received her second Masters in Non-Profit Management. In 2005, Sony Pictures and MGM merged, and Jason went to work for Sony, where he is currently an Executive Vice President.

Jason and Laurie have a son, Wes, who is a senior in high school, and a daughter, Sylvie, who is in the ninth grade. Wes is a debater, musician, and basketball player. Sylvie is involved in the theater, both as a performer and behind the scenes.

Elissa Spivak Marshall

My daughter Elissa was born June 1970. She was a beautiful baby girl and grew up to be a beautiful woman, both inside and out. Lis, as I call her, was a very active little girl and began walking when she was nine months old. She also loved animals and would not leave us alone until we got a dog, and in the years since, she has always had a dog.

Lis was a very good student, got along well with her teachers, and played sports. When she was 10 years old, I coached her Little League team. Lis was one of two girls on the team, played third base, and was one of the team's best players. At age 11 she played on the girls' basketball team at Oakwood Secondary School. By the time she was 12 she got into horses, which ended her baseball career—she would rather ride horses than eat! This love of animals followed her through her entire life.

After high school, Lis went to college in San Diego, then left to enter the entertainment industry where she worked as an assistant for Steve Tisch, an Academy Award-winning film producer. She also worked with film producer Wendy Finerman on music scores for feature films.

All in the Family

When Lis was about 20 years old, a friend invited. her to come stay for a week in New York City. One week turned into two years and she worked with Kevin Bray at Hex films in music video production. A few years later, she moved back to Los Angeles and then to San Francisco. Her high school boyfriend, Scott Marshall, came to visit her in San Francisco and convinced Lis to move back to Los Angeles. At that time, they renewed their romance and were married two years later.

Lis and Scott live in Malibu and have three children: Sam 20, Ethan 18, and Emma 16. Sam is currently a junior at Northwestern University where he studies music. Ethan is a freshman at Pomona College, one of the most prestigious universities on the West Coast. Ethan taught himself to speak, write, and read Korean by engaging an online Korean language teacher who teaches school in Seoul, South Korea. Ethan is fluent in several languages and wants to study international languages at Pomona College.

Emma is 16 and a junior at her high school in Malibu, enjoys dance, and is very close with her family.

Elissa is involved in community service and volunteers at the high school. At the end of the 2023 school year when Ethan was graduating, Elissa received the coveted "Honorary Service Award" for exemplary service to the school over the past six years. Scott works in the film industry as a director and teaches Film Production at the New York Film Academy.

Todd Weill

Leslie's son Todd was 16 when Leslie and I first started dating. He is truly one of the sweetest people I know. Todd accepted me from the first time we met.

Todd went to Crossroads, a private high school in Santa Monica close to where we live, and played on the school's varsity baseball team. Baseball was something we had in common. But that wasn't the only thing we shared.

From the time he was a little boy, Todd had learning disabilities very similar to mine and having this understanding of what he was going through brought us closer. Leslie gave him a lot of help and fortunately, the schools were more prepared to help students with learning disabilities in the 1980s.

After high school, Todd went to San Diego State University where he received a scholarship from Kaiser Permanente, a health insurance company. After college, Todd lived in Del Mar, a suburb of San Diego. His first job after graduating from college was working at DonJoy selling knee, and leg braces. He left DonJoy to work for Novartis, a pharmaceutical company, and has been in the medical industry for more than 30 years. In 2008 Novartis moved Todd and his family to Dallas where they live today.

Todd met Deanne Beck in 1993 and three years later they had a beautiful wedding in our backyard. Todd and Deanne have two children: Sydney, 22 and Jack, 20. Sydney graduated from San Diego State University where she majored in English and also tutored students in sign language. She is currently working at a local school in a suburb of Dallas, Texas, where she grew up.

Jack is a junior at the University of Arizona pursuing a Business Administration degree and during summers he comes back home to Dallas and works as a food server at a local Italian restaurant. When Jack was younger, he was a very good baseball player. In high school he was a good student and he was also on the wrestling team.

Dayna Golenberg

Dayna was 14 years old when Leslie and I started dating. She was a typical young girl with lots of friends. She graduated from Palisades High School then attended Arizona State University where she studied Psychology and graduated in three years. She went on to graduate school and received a Master's Degree in Marriage and Family Counseling. Dayna worked as a therapist at a group home for pregnant teenage girls referred to Juvenile Hall and ran groups for Domestic Violence victims. She now teaches pre-school at a Jewish temple.

She and her husband, Jeff Golenberg, have three children: Jordan, 23; Alexandra, 21; and Carly, 14. Jordan graduated from the University of Arizona in Business and works at Creative Artist Agency in Century City, California. His passions are music, guitar, tennis, and pickleball.

Alexandra goes to college and works at a local restaurant. Carly is in high school and enjoys cooking and playing tennis and is looking forward to going to college.

Jeff owns Silver Lining Entertainment, a talent agency that represents actors, directors and producers who are working in film and television. He and Dayna live in Tarzana, California and enjoy concerts, the beach, and traveling with their family.

Chapter 21
Retirement

On February 1, 2016, I "turned off the lights and closed the door" on the last 40 years. I was 73 and had done everything I set out to do in my career—times 34—which is the number of restaurants we now had when I sold my GCI stock to my partner, Chuck Mathewson. I chose John Sola to be my successor and was confident of the company's future with him at the helm. After all, nobody knew the company's philosophy, culture, and operation style better than John.

I have not been into any of our restaurants since that February day. I decided that if I were to visit one and saw something I didn't like, there wouldn't be anything I could do about it. I wanted to remember all 34 restaurants as they were when I last saw them.

My family didn't think I could stop working and live the life of a retired person. Leslie was quite concerned about the decision I had made. What would I do now?

My first call was to Chuck Frank to let him know I was ready to reboot our consulting company, Spivak & Frank, that we started the *first* time I retired from GCI in 2006. I wanted to lease an office but Leslie said no, and turned the room above our garage into a beautiful office space for me. Now I was set for the start of my retirement. When you worked as hard as I did all those years, you just couldn't *stop* working.

Having been the Chairman of the California Restaurant Association, I was already getting calls from fellow restaurateurs wanting advice or just to share ideas. A few people called to talk about how to turn one restaurant into a chain of restaurants. Others wanted to know how to develop their idea into a restaurant concept. I would meet them for lunch, listen to their ideas and share my thoughts. Developing the new concepts is what I liked the most and I surprised myself about how much I had learned about the restaurant business over the last 40 years! I had architects, accounts, construction companies, marketing, and legal people I had worked with in the past and was able to bring all these people together to develop and open new concepts. Leslie was happy I was keeping busy doing meaningful work that I enjoyed, and this kept me occupied for the first couple of years.

Then came COVID-19 in March 2020 and the restaurant business came to a dead stop. Now I was getting calls about how to survive. I advised them to explore the government programs and referred them to someone who had that expertise. Those programs saved many restaurants.

As for me and Leslie, the pandemic changed our lives, but not totally in a bad way. We pretty much stayed home for 18 months. Our days consisted of working out and walking on the treadmill two hours a day. I cooked dinner every night. I also cooked for my daughter Elissa and her family once a week. I would make something and drive it over to her house, which was 45 minutes away. When I arrived, I'd leave the food on the front porch and call her from the driveway. She and her husband and their three children would come to the door and wave. Leslie and I would also drive over to Jason's house, park in the driveway and talk to them from our cell phones as they sat on the front porch. That's the only way we saw the kids for 18 months.

I would drive Leslie to the market and sit in the car with our dog Daily (named after the Daily Grill) while she did all the shopping—we called that "Driving Miss Daisy." During that time, I honed my cooking skills, and each night Leslie and I would take a glass of wine and sit on the front porch and meet all our neighbors we had never met before. The time went faster than we expected.

Now, I get up early, watch the news programs, exercise, and then go to my home office which has a TV and a reclining chair where I do all my "deep" thinking. I answer emails and may meet friends or business associates for lunch. Afternoons I would work on this book, an exercise which sometimes involved staring out the window and watching Daily play in the yard.

At 5 p.m. I would start cooking dinner and after, Leslie and I would watch a show before going to bed. We get up the next day and start all over again. Weekends are for our kids and grandchildren.

One evening in the spring of 2022, our doctor, Clem Yang, and his wife Angie, came to the house for dinner. Angie brought a large basket of home-grown tomatoes, all different sizes and shapes. These tomatoes were better than any I've ever had! When I asked her about them, she told me about Tomatomania®. "What is it?" I asked.

She told me that during the winter, a company grows seedlings of about 50 varieties of tomatoes in a hothouse and sells them at a corn stand near our house. Later, Angie and Clem took us to the corn stand and helped select a dozen different varieties for me to grow at home. Our gardener, Martine, built a cage I could use to grow my tomato plants. Those tomatoes grew beautifully and were ready for harvest in June and July; they were sensational! This brought back memories of growing tomatoes in agricultural class in Van Nuys High School. Leslie and I distribute the surplus tomatoes to people experiencing homelessness on the streets of Los Angeles, just as our high school class did all those years ago.

Retirement is the best part of my life. I'm now 80 years old and I truly never thought I would be as happy as I am. Leslie, family, restaurant friends, the many social friends Leslie and I have made through the years, and writing and cooking are very fulfilling for me.

Over the years, many people have urged me to write my story. Writing has been tremendously satisfying and without my daughter-in-law, Laurie Spivak, this book wouldn't even exist. Several years ago, Laurie had researched my father's career and The Grill on the Alley with the idea of publishing a book and had written several chapters. At that time, I was too busy with all the restaurants to be an active participant and the project was set aside. Now that I'm retired and have the time, I wanted to write about my life. Much of Laurie's earlier work is included in this book.

In early 2022, I started interviewing ghost writers. My plan was to use what Laurie had already written, then build upon that and tell someone my story and have them write it. I talked to several editors and ghost writers, but everyone I talked to wanted me to write about all the celebrities who came into The Grill on the Alley in Beverly Hills. That's not what I wanted. My goal was to write my *life* story: about growing up in my parents' restaurants, my struggles with dyslexia during my school years and how athletics got me through, starting a family and trying to find my way in business, the success I was able to achieve later in life and, of course, the enduring love I found with Leslie.

I searched LinkedIn and found a likely candidate, but he decided the project wasn't right for him and referred me to Thekla Fagerlie-Madsen. I called Thekla and we talked about my project. "I'll tell you my story and you can write it for me," I said.

"That's not the way it works," she said. I had to write my own story—in my own "voice."

"But I didn't get past high school," I told her. "I don't think

I can do it."

"Just start writing," she said. "Don't worry about spelling, punctuation, or grammar. Just write and when you finish a chapter, send it to me."

When I was in school and struggling with learning disabilities, I still had to keep my grades up to stay eligible to play football, so I took Typing, an easy A. By the 12th grade, I was quite good; I didn't know Algebra or Spanish, but I sure knew how to type.

So, I wrote. I started chronologically with the stories my sister and mother would tell me before I was old enough to remember. When I finished a chapter, I'd send it to Thekla. She'd send back the edited copy with comments and questions and then we'd have a conference call to discuss. I really enjoyed those sessions—her questions prompted other stories and details that I had forgotten.

I still struggle with dyslexia, but I'm aware of it now and that has helped. Sometimes when reading a book, I'll get three or four pages past a point before I realize I'm getting lost, and then I'll go back and re-read the section. I have to slow down, which is hard for me to do—it's just not my nature! Despite the dyslexia and lack of a formal secondary education, I feel I've been very lucky and as I walked through the years during the course of writing this book, I remembered many of the people who helped me along the way and the people I'm thankful were in my life.

My father was always proud of me and both of my parents— through their own failures and successes—showed me how to get back on my feet when I got knocked down. Then there were the people along the way who believed in me and provided opportunities, like Maurie Gettleman, my boss and mentor at Fedco Foods and Soup 'n Such.

I think about Mike Weinstock and Richard Shapiro and how different my life would be if we hadn't met that day at the Bel-Air Sands hotel and agreed to become partners in The Grill on the Alley. While a success in its own right, The Grill became a springboard for the Daily Grill, Public School, and other business ventures and partnerships that continued to enrich my life.

I think about how terrific my children are and the relationship I enjoy with Leslie's children.

But clearly, I'm most grateful for reuniting with Leslie, the love of my life and the "blonde" of the title. When I started writing this book, she, more than anyone, made me feel I could tell my story, my way.

I encourage everyone who is reading this—if you're struggling, keep going. Opportunities arise where you least expect them. I believe you just need the basic values of integrity, a good work ethic, the will to succeed, and tenacity; all of which I learned from my parents.

Oh—and one more thing—if you ever find yourself at The Grill on the Alley, try the Chicken Pot Pie.

The Restaurant Business:
An Insider's View

So, You Want to Be in The Restaurant Business

Over the years, I have given more than 100 presentations about the restaurant business. I lecture a class three times a year at UCLA Extension and at The Collins College of Hospitality Management at California Polytechnic State University in Pomona. I've talked to Rotary Clubs, Chambers of Commerce Young Professional Organizations (YPO), restaurant associations, and various other groups.

Everyone wants to know my secret to success.

The secret is; there is no secret and there are no shortcuts. The keys to success are integrity, tenacity, perseverance, and hard work.

This section is for those who want to know more about the business of restaurants; how we raised money, built a culture, and inspired and supported our team members. I hope that the lessons I learned in my restaurant career can be applied in your own life.

Raising Money

Without exception, the most often question asked is, *"How do I raise the money to open my first restaurant?"*

There is only one way I know of: family and friends. (Although it does help to know people like Mike Weinstock and Richard Shapiro!)

It's very difficult to raise the money for a first restaurant venture any other way. Financial institutions are reluctant to loan money to people who don't have a track record in the business or assets to pledge for the loan. Private Equity firms want to see that you have several successful restaurants before they are interested in investing their money with you.

Before you can start asking for money, you need to have something to show people. The first step is to create a Business Plan. The Business Plan is a document that sets out your business goals and how you're going to achieve them.

Before preparing the Business Plan, I recommend consulting an accountant, lawyer, and someone with restaurant experience to ensure your plan has all the necessary components.

Today, I refer people who call me for help to three people:

- Jean Hagan, a partner at KROST Accounting Firm in Los Angeles, specializes in restaurant operations and consulting. (Jean.hagan@krostcpas.com)
- Chuck Frank, my old partner, for help in the northern California region. (Chuck@CAFRestaurants.com)
- Jot Conde, the President and Chief Executive of the California Restaurant Association for general

restaurant industry information.
(jcondie@calrest.org)

The following is an example of business plan components for a restaurant. This is included for illustration only.

1. Executive Summary

This is a brief summary of the Business Plan containing the following elements:

a) Mission Statement
b) General company information
c) Description of concept
d) Execution – how will the concept be completed
e) Financing – current status and/or funding requirements
f) Future funding plans

2. Mission Statement

Our Mission Statement: "Take care of your guests, the team members and your purveyors and the rest will take care of itself."

3. Company Overview

Details about the company you're building: concept, location, customers, business structure

a. Detailed Description of Concept

   i. Style of Service

      1. <u>Full Service</u>: Server taking the order, serving the meal, checking back to make sure everything is what the guest was expecting, refilling drinks, cleaning table after guest is finished eating, offering coffee, taking dessert order, serving dessert, and bringing the bill to the table.

2. <u>Quick Casual:</u> Guest orders meal at the counter and pays at time of ordering, sits at a table. Food runner brings food to the table and that ends the service.

3. <u>Fast Food</u>: Guest orders at the counter gets a number and waits for the food to be ready. Guest picks food up at a counter and takes to a table to eat.

4. <u>Take Out Only:</u> Guest orders at a counter and pays for the food at that time. Guest waits for food to be ready. Most take-out restaurants give you the ability to order online and pick up your orders. Also, take-out only usually has a home or office delivery program.

b. Menu

   i. Every new restaurant needs to have a well-defined concept.

     1. When we opened The Grill, our concept was a "Traditional American Grill," the roots of which came from "grills" in major cities across the US.

     2. We referenced the Tadich Grill, Jacks Grill, and Sam's Grill, which were all in San Francisco, as well as Musso & Frank Grill in Hollywood.

     3. We also researched New York's Toots Shor, 21 Club, and 25 other bars to get the feeling of New York for our restaurant.

   ii. Color pictures of the food

c. Architect and Interior Design

    i. Hire a draft person, architect, or interior designer to do a floor plan and rendering of the proposed space.

        1. Make sure the architect and interior designer have restaurant experience.

            a. Be careful and make sure this is the correct person to do the job you want.

            b. If the architect doesn't have restaurant experience, they won't understand how the dining room interfaces with the kitchen.

            c. Home interior designers may not have restaurant interior design knowledge of materials and fabrics that won't wear well or can't be cleaned.

        2. You can also list their accomplishments in the restaurant field in your brochure.

    ii. Color pictures of the restaurant design rendering.

  d. Location

    i. Describe the real estate broker you are working with.

        1. Include their resume of restaurants they have worked with.

4. Team and Management

  a. Your Experience

    i. Any restaurant experience you may have

    ii. Any other businesses you have owned

      iii. Complete work experience history

      iv. Investment: Potential investors always ask if you are putting your own money into the project.

      v. If you don't have a lot of restaurant experience, it helps to have a restaurant consultant who has done what you are attempting to do.

  b. Management Overview

  c. Staff

  d. Ownership structure

      i. Incorporated

      ii. Limited Liability

      iii. Employee-Owned

      iv. Sole Proprietor

5. Marketing and Sales

  a. Analysis of Industry

  b. Competition

  c. Sales & Other Revenue Streams

      i. Food sales

      ii. Alcohol sales

      iii. Takeout

      iv. Catering

      v. Merchandise sales

6. Financial Projections

Word of Caution: Don't estimate sales and make your projections fit into your estimate. Make sure you can easily support your projections. This is what investors will be basing their investment on.

a. Financial projections must be realistic but optimistic.

    i. Square footage of proposed space or number of seats.

    ii. The average spend in dollars for each guest.

        1. Including alcohol if part of your concept.

    iii. Estimate how many times a seat will get used during the various meal periods.

        1. Calculated by using points and (a)(ii) above.

        2. If your restaurant is going to be open lunch and dinner you might start with Monday using ½ of the seats for lunch and dinner.

            a. Tuesday builds up to 60%

            b. Wednesday 80%

            c. Thursday 100%

            d. Friday and Saturday 150%

            e. Sunday 100%.

        3. Then multiply then number of covers (guests seated) to come up with the estimated volume per week, month, or year.

            a. Best to give 3 different scenarios with the projection you came up with:

                i. Breakeven

                ii. Most likely –

                    1. You have a restaurant that ends up with a 15 percent cash flow against sales.

        2. Determine how much business is needed to keep the rent at 5 to 8 percent of sales

    iii. Best Case - 150% of projection

b. Profit and Loss Proforma

    i. *You always use Cash Flow, not Profit for the return.* Profit includes non-cash items like depreciation. Cash flow is more meaningful as it is the total sales less the actual restaurant expenses.

    ii. Demonstrate the amount of cash flow your restaurant can generate.

        1. Cash Flow equals: Sales Less Cost of Goods Sold (COGS):

            a. Labor Costs:

                i. Your salary

                ii. Employee salaries

                iii. Employee benefits

            b. Variable and Fixed Costs:

                i. Utilities

                ii. Linen

                iii. Cleaning supplies

                iv. Insurance

            c. Miscellaneous Expenses:

                i. Replacement of dishes, glasses, pots, pans

                ii. Computer supplies

        iii. Paper goods

        iv. Repairs and Maintenance

   d. Taxes

   e. Occupancy cost including all leasehold extras:

        i. Rent and rent related expenses such as:

        ii. Property taxes

        iii. Repairs and maintenance

        iv. Insurance

c. Budget: how much money you need to complete the project.

    i. Legal fees

    ii. Architectural fees

    iii. Interior Design fees

    iv. Kitchen Design fees

    v. Construction (as a percentage of square footage and number of seats)

    vi. Equipment

    vii. Signage

    viii. Training

    ix. Pre-opening costs

        1. Employee training

        2. Food for cook training

x. Opening Inventory

xi. Smallwares (kitchen utensils)

xii. Pots, pans, and all cooking equipment.

xiii. Dishes, flatware

xiv. Table accessories

xv. Computer systems

xvi. POS Equipment (point of sale computer)

xvii. Working Capital

NOTE: This information is an overview; more information may need to be included in official documents to raise funds. I recommend consulting an accountant and a lawyer when preparing documents to present to potential investors.

Once this information is compiled and prepared for presentation, you're ready to raise the necessary funds.

Remember, banks will not be interested. SBA (Small Business Administration) will only be helpful if you have some real estate assets to pledge. Be careful about this. You don't want to lose your house because your restaurant didn't work.

Deal Structure

The first few restaurants we operated under a Limited Partnership model which allowed me to raise funds and the investor liability was solely limited to the extent of their investment. You, as a General Partner, are liable for the debts of the venture.

You can also incorporate, which we did in subsequent years by forming Grill Concepts, Inc. That way, the corporation is the responsible party. Incorporation protects you from the liability of a General Partner.

In a Limited Partnership, the investors don't have any say in how you run your business, but they do expect a return on their investment. Ideally, it is best if all the capital is returned in 30 months or less.

I usually structured the return to receive a fair salary for running the restaurant, which would be what restaurant General Managers make on average. The investor would receive 90% of the cash flow and I'd get 10% until the investor(s) got their investment back in full.

Once the investor(s) have their investment back, the split goes 40% to investor and 60% to the General Partner (you). It's important to get the investor(s) their investment returned as soon as possible. *This is what the investor is most interested in.* It may seem unfair for the investor to get 90% of the cashflow but, just remember, if you don't raise the money, you won't ever be in the restaurant business. Also, a happy investor will invest again with you if you want to grow your concept.

This is pretty much the way we raised the money to open The Grill on the Alley in Beverly Hills. Nobody knew who I was. The money came from Richard and Mike's friends and family. This is about the only way to get a new venture going without having a track record.

Once you have your first restaurant open, successful, and all investors' capital returned, raising money can be easier because now you have a track record and the investor(s) knows you. In the case of The Grill, we paid all the capital back in 16 months. Then, our investors received 40% of the cash flow for as long as the lease ran, or we sold or bought them out. That's why the 90/10 formula is preferred.

For the opening of the first Daily Grill, we set up the

corporation, Grill Concepts, Inc., into which the investors invested, and were able to raise the necessary funds in three weeks. Those investors owned 10% of the company going forward. Eighteen months later that first Daily Grill was so successful that we raised enough funds to build two more Daily Grills and we were off and running. Once we had those two very successful restaurants, the landlords from shopping malls were offering all sorts of deals.

We opened the second Daily Grill on La Cienega and Beverly Boulevard with investor money. The third Daily Grill was in Newport Beach and the landlord gave us most of the capital to build the restaurant in Fashion Island. The fourth and fifth Daily Grills were in Encino and Studio City and again, the landlords gave us "Tenant Improvement" money to build both of those restaurants. The sixth Daily Grill was in Palm Desert and the seventh in Irvine California, both of which also received very large Tenant Improvement funds to help build them. Now we had seven Daily Grills plus The Grill on the Alley.

We then felt it was important to open a Daily Grill in another city and we chose Washington D.C. because their demographics were very similar to Los Angeles. To do that we had to raise additional capital due to the fact nobody knew us there and we couldn't command large Tenant Improvement dollars.

One of the members of our Board of Directors with extensive financial experience thought we were ready to go public. He found a small, public restaurant company in New Jersey and thought it would be good for us to merge into that company. They owned several Pizzeria Uno franchise restaurants. Through this transaction, which now made us a public company, we were able to raise enough capital to buy the franchise company and open four more Daily Grills in the Washington D.C. area.

However, by 2002 the 107th congress passed the Sarbanes-Oxley Act which made it very expensive for small public companies like ours to raise capital through public offerings.

The Act required public companies to adopt stricter internal procedures to ensure the accuracy of financial statements and made the CEO and CFO of a company directly responsible for the truthfulness, documentation, and submission of financial reports. The additional requirements for disclosure and internal controls dictated by the Act made it harder for smaller companies to raise public funds, but, despite this, we stayed public for several more years and slowed our growth to opening just one restaurant a year through the cash flow we were generating.

We needed to get creative to open additional restaurants.

The hotel expansion helped us do that.

My Management Philosophy & Style

We take care of our Guests
Respect our Team Members
The rest takes care of itself

The first real management decision I remember making was when I worked at the Redwood. I was about 22 years old at the time and there was a kitchen cook who nobody could get along with. He had a big ego, which was not unusual in the restaurant business. If a guest didn't like something and the server returned the meal to the kitchen, this cook would take it as a personal affront and refuse to remake the dish. The server would have to go back and tell the guest we couldn't remake it, which didn't reflect well on our restaurant.

This behavior went against my father's philosophy that "the guest is always right even when they're wrong," a philosophy which also became my own. There's no profit in making the guest wrong.

My father was on vacation and that night, a guest sent their meal back to the kitchen and the cook refused to remake the dish. I felt I needed to deal with the situation. The cook worked until 10 p.m. and since I was at home having dinner, I'd have to drive the 45 minutes back to the restaurant in order to terminate him after his shift. I was very nervous, but knew this was something I had to do, especially if I wanted the respect of the rest of the team. When I told the cook he was no longer needed, he didn't understand what I was talking about. I realized then I should have sat down with him and told him why I made this decision. This was something I hadn't prepared for. I became upset and told him he was fired and to "get out" of the restaurant.

This certainly wasn't the way my father would have handled it. He would have taken this man aside and explained that he had been warned about his behavior several times and had now just crossed a line from which there was no return, and then fired him.

Now, my dad had a short temper. He wanted everything a certain way – his way. He was fair, but firm, and knew how to get the best out of people. The Redwood probably had about 75 people working there. It's hard to have a relationship with that many people, but my dad was "inclusive" in his management style before "inclusive" became a buzzword. He allowed people time for their families, hosted holiday dinners, and would always listen if someone had a problem. People wanted to please him. When he got upset with someone, they would be upset with themselves for somehow letting my father down, rather than getting upset at my father.

I never forgot how badly I handled that first situation. When my dad came back to the restaurant and I told him what happened, he was still proud that I took action because he knew this cook was disruptive and needed to go. Over time, my management philosophy developed into the three-sentence statement at the beginning of this chapter and I adopted my father's "fair but firm" management style.

It wasn't until years later that I learned the proper way to manage people began with the first interview.

The Interview

The interview is a delicate dance. First, you need to understand the person interviewing *wants* the job.

I would always start by just talking about things that had nothing to do with the job to ease the tension. I'd tell them I knew that interviews could be nerve wracking, then I'd ask questions like: How did you get here today? Was there a lot of traffic? Do you have brothers and sisters? Where did you grow up?

By showing an interest in their background, it would hopefully put them at ease. Also, you could learn a lot about someone without asking the obvious questions.

Then I might say something about myself: where I grew up or how I got into the restaurant business.

Next, I'd ask questions to find out what kind of a worker they are, like: What hours do you like to work? Do you have any other time commitments?

If it's a management job, I always ask how many hours a week they would like to work. The answer I always like to hear is "It doesn't matter, I just like to work until the job is done." Or they might say, "I go to school at night and therefore I need to work in the day during the week, but I can work any hours on the weekends."

I always ask them to bring a resume. At this point, I might go through their resume, again keeping in mind they want a job and therefore, they are going to make every job they had sound like a positive experience. I'll take them through each job on their resume and ask why they left. You can learn a lot from how they answer that question. While they probably won't tell you if they were fired, they might say they had a disagreement with their manager. They might have had five jobs in the last four years, and you start wondering why they keep leaving. I always ask if I can call the previous employer or manager for a reference. The chances are they are not going to have you call someone who didn't like them. At that point they might say, "He isn't going to give me a great reference because we didn't get along." I'll ask them to explain why.

If it's full-time employment they are looking for, I always tell them, "I realize this may be a means to an end, that you are studying to be something else, and when that opportunity comes along, I want you to take it. But until then, my goal is that this will be the last job you will ever have in the restaurant industry."

Many servers in Los Angeles want to be actors. For those applicants, I always let them know that the Daily Grill was the last job David Schwimmer had before he got the role of Ross in the television series "Friends." I tell them how David asked me for the day off so he could audition for the role and that we would work around their audition schedules whenever possible.

Always Check References

Checking references is extremely important. The goal is to have the potential employee stay as long as they can. It's very expensive to replace employees. There is the cost of recruiting, training, the time it takes until they get good at the job, and the cost of lost customers because new employees may not be so good at their job quite yet. Also, with the labor laws the way they are today, you can be sued for terminating a person without good cause.

Employee Handbook

You can't hold someone responsible for a job if they don't know all the rules. A good employee handbook:

- Outlines job duties, employer expectations, and code of conduct.
- Helps protect employers in case of legal disputes.
- Is critical to compliance with state and Federal laws.

It's not enough just to give it to the employee, you also want to make sure the employee signs that he or she has read and understands the Handbook.

Training

A person can't do a good job if they don't know what is expected of them. You need to have a training manual.

- Each job description should be accompanied by a written test to make sure the trainee understands their responsibilities.
- The person doing the training should be one of your best employees.
- That trainer should get paid extra for doing this job.

We would train managers for three weeks before we left them alone to run a shift. Cooks were trained for 10 days and servers for eight days. The last three or four days we let the trainee work all the functions while the trainer shadowed them. When training servers, the trainer always let the guest know the new team member would take their order and the trainer was standing by to help them if needed. This provides transparency with the guest.

Follow Up

This may be the most important function of all to have successful team members. Human beings are made to break rules. I don't know about you, but I don't always drive at the speed limit. What keeps me from going too much over the speed limit is the vision of red and blue police lights in my rearview mirror. If a team member is not doing a good job, it's up to management to sit down with them and tell them what they are doing wrong.

I would approach the situation like this:

"Jeanine, you do x and y well but for you to be successful at your job, z needs to change."

This way, you've first acknowledged the things they do well and then provided direction on what needs to change. If they break the rules again you need to put it in writing and again let them know their behavior must change if they wish to continue with their job and that any further poor behavior could result in their termination. If they continue to break the rules, then the team member has essentially terminated themselves.

The "Bob Talk"

Whenever we opened a new restaurant, I would give what the team called "The Bob Talk," a 30-minute talk to all the new team members of the new restaurant(s) we were getting ready to open. I wanted the new team members to understand our concept, mission, and values straight from the founder and CEO of Grill Concepts. I would open with some general industry statistics then take questions. By the end, most of the staff believed they were joining a special restaurant company. The Bob Talk goes something like this:

The Bob Talk

- The restaurant industry is the largest employer in the US.
- 35% of the work force under 40 years of age got their first job in a restaurant.
- The average employee turnover in the industry is 120%. Ours is under 45%.

At Grill Concepts, team members are very important to us. We believe "If we take care of the guests and take care of the team members, the rest will take care of itself."

We recognize there are different reasons why people work in a restaurant:

- To some of you, this may be a means to an end.
- You have other priorities in your life
- School
- Acting
- Sales
- You have a day job that doesn't pay enough yet.
- We will be sensitive to your other priorities.

- We'll listen to your schedule needs.
- All we ask is that you give us 110% when you're here.

Others of you are career restaurant people. We offer:

- A professionally run restaurant.
- Good work environment.
- A company large enough to make sure your paycheck will clear the bank and small enough for you to be heard at every level of management.
- Health insurance for you and your family.

For those people who don't have a career path, we offer opportunity:

- Great training.

- Opportunity for advancement:

  o Most of our chefs started with us as dishwashers or prep cooks.

  o Several of our managers started as servers.

We have a great record of longevity:

After The Grill was open 27 years, 13 people who started with us were still with the company. It would have been 14 but Abel, a busser, retired after 27 years at the age of 72. We gave him a retirement party and the entire staff of 85 people came to wish him a long successful retirement. The servers got together and bought Abel a $200 Stetson cowboy hat. When he put it on, he was so proud it made the entire party a success.

One of the other 13 people still with the company after 27 years was Frankie Espinosa. Frankie worked for my father at the Redwood. He came to work as a non-English speaking

Saved By A Blonde & A Chicken Pot Pie

busser after crossing the border from Mexico at age 18. After Frankie became more fluent in English, I taught him how to tend bar. When we opened The Grill, he came to work as a bartender and eventually became the night manager.

These are just two of the hundreds of people who worked with Grill Concepts until they retired, finished school, or got jobs in the industries they were training for.

Actor David Schwimmer worked at the Daily Grill until he got his dream job as one of the stars on the TV show "Friends." We actually covered David's shift the day he went for the audition.

Several people in Senior Positions have grown up with the company:

- Bart McPhail - started as a trainer and became Regional Area Director (12 years)
- Jim Snodgrass - Regional Area Director (13 years)
- Arthur Meola - Started as manager at The Grill and is now Area Director all The Grill on the Alley restaurants (13 years)
- Israel Camacho - Started on the broiler when we opened. Now he's the Head Chef at The Grill on the Alley in Beverly Hills (40 years)
- Maria Garcia – Started in the pantry making salads and became the Head Chef at The Grill on the Alley in Westlake (26 years)
- Louie Feinstein - started as General Manager, rose to Vice President of Operations (19 years)
- John Sola - started as Head Chef, rose to Senior Vice President of Culinary, and then CEO of Grill Concepts, Inc. until he retired (35 years)

Why do people stay with us?

- We are fair employers (we live by the rules).
- We follow the spirit, not just the letter of the law.
- We value people.
- We make health insurance available to all full-time hourly employees.
- We are proud restaurant people working with proud restaurant workers.

Mission Statement:

We take care of our Guests
Respect our Team Members
The rest takes care of itself

Operating Statement

F.R.E.D. - **F**riendliest **R**estaurant **E**very **D**ay **Our operations are founded on two principals:**

1. The Guest Is Always Right even when they are wrong.

There is no profit in making a guest wrong. We just listen and do everything we can to please them.

2. The answer is yes what is the question?

We don't have any rules that pertain to our valued guests.

- Every person working in restaurant MUST acknowledge every single guest they come in contact with.
  - I'm asking all managers to remind each and every team member to do so.
- Area directors will be reminding managers.

- Host or hostess is the first person who comes in contact with our guests.

  o You only get one chance to make a good first impression. A smile will go a long way.

- Host or Hostess must come out from behind the podium.

  o When you stand behind the podium it creates a barrier between you and your guest.

- We will do just about anything to satisfy a guest.

Marketing people will tell you it costs 10 times as much to market to get a new guest as it does to get a current guest to come in one more time a month.

This story about Mrs. Price will demonstrate how far I will go to satisfy a guest.

Mrs. Price called me on the phone; irate. Her daughter had read about The Grill and the celebrities who ate there and told her mother that the only thing she wanted for her 21st birthday was to eat at The Grill in Beverly Hills. Mrs. Price said she made the reservation six weeks in advance to make sure they got a good table. Then she told me that not only did they *not* get a good table but the restaurant had lost their reservation.

It took 45 minutes to get them seated and another 30 minutes for the server to take their order. When they finally got their food, the daughter's steak was overcooked and everything was cold. Just about everything that could go wrong *did* go wrong.

After about 10 minutes of Mrs. Price ranting about how awful their experience was, she stopped. (I had been trained to let people vent their entire experience before answering.) I said,

"Well Mrs. Price, we really messed this up didn't we. I have no excuse. All I can do is let you know how sorry I am. What can I do to make this up to you?"

She said, "There is nothing you can do, Mr. Spivak. I will never come into your restaurant again."

I said, "Well Mrs. Price, you took the time to let me know what a terrible experience you and your daughter had, and I'd like to make it up to you."

Again, she said, "Don't bother. I'll never come into your restaurant again."

Now, I don't know how I came up with this idea but I said, "You won't let me give you anything, so I'd like to make a donation, in your name, to your favorite charity."

I could hear the change in her voice, and she said, "Mr. Spivak, I'm Jewish and I belong to a very poor Synagogue. I can't turn down a donation to my Temple."

I said, "Mrs. Price, give me the address of the Temple and the name of your Rabbi and I'll make sure the Rabbi knows this donation is made in your name."

She answered, "Bob (now I was Bob) this would be lovely of you, but Bob, you have to do one favor for me."

"What would that be?" I asked.

She said, "You can't tell the Rabbi we were eating in your restaurant! We keep kosher."

Now, Mrs. Price probably won't eat in our restaurant again but how many people do you think she has told this story to?

The lesson here is I don't want any team member to be in a position of denying service to anyone and that I will go to great lengths to satisfy a guest—even knowing they would never be back. It's just good business to leave everyone happy.

Value Statement (Acronym for People)

- **Pride** - Be proud of everything you do in life. People like people who are proud of themselves.

- **Excellent** - Be excellent at everything you do. It doesn't cost one cent more to do a great job as it does to just get by.

- **Opportunity** - At Grill Concepts there is a lot of opportunity, as evidenced by the people who have continued their careers with us.

- **Profit** – This does not have to be a dirty word. It's the profits from our restaurants that allow us to open more restaurants and create more opportunity for our valued team members.

- **Leadership** - You don't have to be CEO of a restaurant company to be a leader. You can be a leader with your family or your friends. Strive to be a leader in everything you do.

- **Enjoyment** - If you don't enjoy what you are doing, go find a job you love. It's hard to be great and have pride in what you do if you're not enjoying the job.

I am proud of Grill Concepts and confident that all of you will have a successful experience working with us as long as you follow the management concepts I have laid out today. I ask those of you who have had several jobs in restaurants if you ever worked for a company who valued you the way we value people. To be a great employer you must be willing to listen to what people have to say. Now, this is your chance to ask any questions. All of you are experienced restaurant workers. I ask you to let me know anything any of your former employers did that you think could make us a better restaurant company. Please don't be afraid or intimidated to speak up.

End of The Bob Talk

Lessons Learned

Throughout the years, people I've worked with have said things to me which I've never forgotten. While some of these stories have already been told, I think the lessons are important enough to repeat them here.

All In a Day's Work

When I was working in the foods department at Fedco Discount Store one night, my manager was cleaning the peanut butter machine. This was a very messy job as the oil from the peanuts clogged up the grinder. I didn't think that as manager, he should be doing this dirty job. I said to him, "Norman, you're the manager. Let me do that for you."

He said, "It's all in a day's work."

I was so impressed with his answer that I never forgot it.

Follow Me

While still working at Fedco, the head of all the meat departments for the six stores said to me, "If you are in a war and there is shooting going on and the commander wants to move the troops from one point to another, there is only one command he can say to get his soldiers to risk their lives, and that is FOLLOW ME!"

In another words, when you are managing people and you want them to do something new, the best way is to show them.

Command Respect - Don't Demand It

When I was the CEO of Grill Concepts, Inc. with over 2,000 team members, I still asked everyone to call me Bob. If they call me Mr. Spivak, it puts me on a different level. If they call me Bob, we are the same. They know who is in charge; I don't have to constantly remind them.

All Customers are Guests

I want all the people who come into our restaurant to be treated like guests in your own home. Therefore, we refer all our customers as guests.

It's Not What You Say but How You Say It

My mother used to say, "It's not what you say, it's how you say it." When team members make a mistake or break the rules, speak to them with respect. There's no need to get mad, yell, or be upset. Just be respectful—even if reprimanding or correcting a team member.

Communication

I can't stress enough the importance of talking with people. Email and texting are fine to set up a meeting or answer a question, but it's not a substitute for talking to someone. Communication is two-way; texting is only one way. I would sit with the crew while they were eating the team member dinner and just chat with everyone. You'd be surprised how much you can learn to make the restaurant better in this casual atmosphere.

A Lesson in Generosity of Spirit - The Jim Collins Story

"How did you get into the restaurant business?" I asked Jim Collins, the Founder of the Collins College of Hospitality Management, as we drove to Pomona for a board meeting. It was 1995 and at that time I'd been on the Board of the Collins College for eight years but when I picked Jim up, I wasn't sure what we would talk about for the hour-long drive. I needn't have worried; his answer took up most of the ride.

Jim graduated from UCLA as an engineer in 1949. His father-in-law owned a trailer park on the corner of Centinela Avenue and Sepulveda Boulevard in Culver City and Jim recounted how his father-in-law knew that if he had a restaurant on the property, it would enhance the value of his trailer park. Since Jim had an engineering degree, his father-in-law thought he could build a restaurant. Jim was about to embark on a venture that would change his life.

Jim talked to one of his friends who invited him to come with him to San Bernardino, which was a two-hour drive in those days. When they got to San Bernadino, they went to a restaurant named McDonald's which sold 15-cent hamburgers. They arrived to a line of people stretched around the block waiting to order a McDonald's hamburger. Jim was so amazed he brought his father-in-law to San Bernadino to see the place where people waited in line over an hour for a hamburger.

Jim and his father-in-law went back to Culver City and built a 19-cent hamburger quick service restaurant in the trailer park they called Hamburger Handout, patterned after McDonald's. Hamburger Handout was just as busy as McDonald's with lines stretching two city blocks long every day at noon.

Soon, other business people were coming from all over the U.S. to see the phenomenon of the 15- and 19-cent hamburgers. Jim, being a friendly and helpful person, would help these people open their own hamburger stands in their cities.

One day, Pete Harman, Jim's friend who lived in Salt Lake City, Utah, called to let Jim know about the fried chicken he was selling at his hamburger restaurant. Pete told Jim that a man from Kentucky who called himself Colonel Sanders came to his back door with a recipe for fried chicken that had 11 herbs and spices. Pete insisted Jim come to Salt Lake City and try the chicken. Jim did, and was very impressed with the product.

Jim and Pete flew to Lexington, Kentucky to meet the Colonel and the rest is history. Pete was the first franchise owner for Colonel Sanders Kentucky Fried Chicken, or KFC as it's widely known as now. Jim also opened a KFC in Southern California. Jim later secured Southern California and Australia for the master franchise. After opening three KFCs in the Los Angeles area and seeing the tremendous reception they got, Jim knew he was on to something. He found someone to lease Hamburger Handout and focused on expanding his chicken franchise to Australia. After opening about 50 KFC restaurants, the man who was leasing the Hamburger Handout from Jim's father-in-law called Jim to let him know he was going to retire and give up the restaurant. Jim said, "That's my father-in-law's trailer park. The restaurant has to stay open."

The man replied, "Come pick up the key because I'm going to close the place."

Jim went straight away to the trailer park. The man told Jim he was selling $1.29 steak dinners and the restaurant was called Sizzler. In three years, he had made enough money to retire. Well, Jim realized there was a big market for Sizzler. He decided to open more of the Sizzler's as well as more KFC's and in 1968 he formed a company named Collins Foods Inc.

In 2016 there were 217 restaurants in Australia and 65 in Asia. The company had 9,200 employees as well as 270 Sizzler restaurants throughout the 11 Western states and in Australia. All of Jim's success came from the Hamburger Handout restaurant he had built for his father-in-law and the subsequent relationships developed from helping others to establish their own businesses.

Needless to say, that one-hour drive went very fast and I learned a valuable lesson from Jim about helping people without asking anything in return. From that day forward, I never turned anyone down who asked for my help.

A few years later, Jim Collins called and wanted me to meet him for breakfast in the coffee shop of the hotel on the northwest corner of Slauson Avenue and Sepulveda Boulevard in Culver City to discuss hiring a new Dean at Collins College. While we were eating breakfast and going through the candidate resumes, I told Jim I was going to the restroom. But what I really wanted was to find the server and give her my credit card so she wouldn't bring the check to the table. Jim was so generous that he always paid whenever we were out together, and I didn't want him to do so this time.

When we were through with our meeting and ready to leave, Jim called the server over and asked for the check. The server told him I had taken care of it. Jim looked at me and said, "Bob, why did you pay for breakfast? I own this hotel!" The next time we met for breakfast, I let Jim take care of the check.

My dad was still alive when Jim started his restaurant empire and admired Jim's accomplishments. Even though my dad passed away over 30 years ago, I like to think he would be proud to know that Jim Collins, an icon in our industry, is a friend of mine.

Recipes

Bloody Mary Mix

Serves 8

Ingredients:

1 can tomato juice (46 ounce) (premium brand such as Campbell's recommended)

2 teaspoons ground black pepper

1 teaspoon celery salt

½ cup Worcestershire sauce

2 lemons, juiced

2 teaspoons celery seed

2 teaspoons salt

8 stalks celery for garnish

3 fresh limes, cut into 6 wedges each for juice and garnish

1 dashes Tabasco sauce (optional)

Preparation Method:

1. Mix all ingredients together, except limes and celery.
2. Fill a 12 to 16 ounce glass ¾ full with ice cubes.
3. Add 2 ounces vodka (any vodka will work).
4. Fill the rest of the glass with the Bloody Mary Mix.
5. Squeeze the juice of one lime wedge in and stir well with celery stalk.
6. Garnish with new lime wedge and celery stalk.
7. Optional Garnish: Toothpick with green olive or pepperoncini.

Bloody Mary mix can be stored in refrigerator for up to one week.

Bob's Hint: Don't drink all 8 yourself!

Bobby's Special Dry Rub

Use this rub for BBQ or Smoking when a recipe calls for a dry rub on Brisket, Tri-tip, Ribs, Pork Loin, etc.

<u>Ingredients:</u>

2 Tablespoons Kosher salt

1 Tablespoon garlic powder

1 Tablespoon ground black pepper

1 Tablespoon Old Bay Seasoning

2 Tablespoons smoked paprika

1 Tablespoon dried oregano

1 Tablespoon onion powder

1 teaspoon cayenne pepper

<u>Preparation Method:</u>

1. Mix above ingredients thoroughly and store in a shaker.

2. The day before cooking, apply liberally on all sides of the meat.

3. Wrap the meat tightly in plastic wrap.

4. Refrigerate overnight.

5. Take meat out of refrigerator 1 hour before smoking or grilling to bring to room temperature.

Note: You can add 3 tablespoons vegetable oil to make this a 'wet' rub.

Bob's Hint: All meats cook better when you take them out of the refrigerator and let rest for 1 hour before cooking.

Caesar Salad

Serves 4

<u>Lettuce/Crouton Ingredients:</u>

3 small Romaine hearts (use ONLY light color leaves) Cut across the leaves - about 1-inch strips

2 slices sourdough bread

2 Tablespoons Extra Virgin Olive Oil (EVOO)

Kosher salt & ground black pepper

<u>Crouton Preparation Method:</u>

1. Cut 2 slices of sourdough bread into ½ inch squares.
2. Toss bread cubes with EVOO, salt and pepper.
3. Toast in a 400-degree oven until light brown on all sides (about 5 minutes).

<u>Dressing Ingredients and Preparation Method:</u>

2 cloves garlic, minced fine

2 Tablespoons fresh lemon juice

1 teaspoon anchovy (minced) or anchovy paste (1/2 fillet)

1 teaspoon Dijon mustard

1 teaspoon Worcestershire sauce

¼ teaspoon ground black pepper

¼ teaspoon Kosher salt

1 cup mayonnaise (high-quality brand recommended)

2 Tablespoons water

1 cup Parmigiano Reggiano (aged 24 months)

Recipes

1. Place all ingredients in bowl, except Parmigiano, and whisk all together.

2. When well-blended, add ½ cup Parmigiano and mix again.

<u>Salad Assembly:</u>

1. Toss cut lettuce in the dressing until well coated.

2. Add Croutons and remaining Parmigiano and toss a few more times.

3. Top with fresh cracked black pepper.

Papa Eddie's Bouillabaisse

This recipe was made famous at Pappa Eddie's Bouillabaisse restaurant described in this book.

Serves 10

<u>Ingredients:</u>

1-½ pounds shrimp (21-25 per pound), peeled, deveined and tail off

1 pound sea bass (deboned and cut into cubes)

1 pound red snapper (deboned and cut into cubes)

1 -½ pounds Dungeness crab legs (approximately 15 legs) cut into 2-inch segments

2 dozen Littleneck clams, scrubbed clean

2 Tablespoons Extra Virgin Olive Oil (EVOO)

3 onions, large (sliced thin)

2 red peppers (chopped - no seeds or pith)

4 branches celery (chopped)

4 carrots (cut in half length-wise, sliced into ¼-inch half-moons)

4 cloves garlic (minced)

4 cans (28-ounce) stewed tomatoes (San Marzano preferred)

4 bay leaves

2 lemons (juice only)

1 teaspoon Saffron threads

2 cans (48-ounce) Ocean Clam Juice

2 cans (6-1/2 ounce) clams (chopped, in juice)

1 cup dry sherry

Kosher salt and fresh ground black pepper

2 Tablespoons fresh parsley (1 bunch finely chopped for garnish)

<u>Preparation Method:</u>

1. In large stock pot, heat olive oil and cook onions, red pepper, celery, carrots, garlic, bay leaves, and salt and pepper until the vegetables are soft and begin to brown, stirring often.

2. Add stewed tomatoes, lemon juice, and saffron and simmer for 30 minutes.

3. Add clam juice and bring to a boil

4. Add sea bass and cook for 15 minutes.

5. Add red snapper and cook for an additional five minutes.

6. Remove fish from stock, and cook shrimp 2 minutes until shrimp are pink. **Don't overcook!**

7. Remove shrimp and reserve to the side.

8. Add crabs and clams and cook until clams open.

9. Add back remaining fish and cook for 5 minutes, but continue to reserve shrimp.

10. Add sherry and serve over the shrimp.

11. Garnish with chopped parsley.

12. Serve with Rouille on the side.

13. Add Kosher salt and fresh ground black pepper as needed, for taste.

(Reserve 3 Tablespoons of this Bouillabaisse Broth for Rouille preparation.)

For Plating: Distribute seafood evenly in 10 warm bowls.

Cover with Bouillabaisse broth.

Garnish with fresh chopped parsley. Serve with Rouille on the side.

Bob's Hint: Chef should be wearing a beret while cooking for true South-of-France taste.

Rouille

Ingredients:

¾ teaspoon Saffron threads

1 Tablespoons Bouillabaisse broth

2 Tablespoons bread crumbs (fine, plain)

¼ teaspoon dried red chili flakes

3 cloves garlic, small (chopped fine)

1/8 teaspoon Kosher salt

1 egg yolk

¾ cup Extra Virgin Olive Oil (EVOO)

Preparation Method:

1. Steep saffron in 3 Tablespoons of Bouillabaisse Broth to 'bloom' the threads.
2. Add bread crumbs to saffron mix and purée in food processor.
3. Add chili flakes, garlic and salt.
4. Add egg yolk and pulse until blended and smooth.
5. Add EVOO (in a stream) while food processor is mixing (30 seconds to add oil).
6. Remove from processor and refrigerate.

Note: Mixture should be the consistency of mayonnaise.

Gazpacho

Serves 4-6

First Day

Ingredients:

4 tomatoes, large, ripe (peeled and seeded)

3 cucumbers, medium (peeled and seeded)

½ yellow onion, small (diced)

4 ounces water

1 cup tomato juice (premium brand - Campbell's recommended)

1 Tablespoon Extra Virgin Olive Oil (EVOO)

1 clove garlic, small (chopped fine)

1 Tablespoon dried oregano

¼ teaspoon ground cumin

1 Avocado, medium, ripe (diced for garnish)

Preparation Method:

1. Using double-edge blade of food processor, combine tomatoes, cucumbers, and onions.
2. Pulse to keep chunky, about 10 pulses.
3. Add water, tomato juice, EVOO, garlic and spices.
4. Mix well by hand and refrigerate for 24 hours.

Second Day

Ingredients:

1 cup Tomato Juice (premium brand - Campbell's - recommended)

1 Tablespoon Worcestershire sauce

1 Tablespoon red wine vinegar

1 teaspoon hot sauce (more or less, to taste)

¾ Tablespoon Kosher salt

1 lemon, juiced (2 ounces)

½ teaspoon ground black pepper

Preparation Method:

1. Mix-in above ingredients with ingredients prepared the first day.

2. Top with diced avocado.

3. Drizzle with additional EVOO and serve cold.

Bob's Hint: I like mine spicey. Leslie likes hers mild. Guess which one I make? I add more hot sauce to my bowl.

Chicken Vegetable Soup

Serves 6 Bowls or 12 Cups

Stock

Ingredients:

- 1 whole chicken (approximately 4 pounds)
- 2 quarts chicken broth (recommend: Costco Bone Broth)
- 2 quarts water
- 1 onion, medium sized, cut into quarters
- 3 cloves garlic, minced
- 2 cups carrots, sliced into ½ inch chunks (for stock)
- 1 teaspoon black whole peppercorns
- 2 stalks celery, sliced into ½ inch chunks (save tops for stock)
- 2 Tablespoons fresh parsley (chopped) (chop 6 stems separately for stock)
- 3 bay leaves
- 1 sprig fresh thyme

Preparation Method:

1. Add whole chicken to large stock pot and cover with chicken broth and water (add more water if necessary to make sure chicken is covered.)
2. Add remaining stock ingredients. Bring to boil, then immediately reduce to low simmer.
3. Cook for 1 hour, until internal chicken temperature reaches 165 degrees F.
4. Turn off heat – let chicken rest in seasoned broth for 20 minutes.

5. Remove chicken from broth, saving any meat that falls off the bone.

6. Strain broth into large bowl, discard leaves, stems, etc.

7. Chill chicken and broth separately in refrigerator.

8. Skim fat off chilled broth.

9. Pull chicken from bones leaving in large pieces - throw away skin, bones, fat and scraps.

Soup

<u>Ingredients:</u>

1 onion, medium, cut into ½-inch pieces

1 carrot, medium, cut into ½-inch wheels

1 leek, medium, washed, cut length-wise, then cut into ¼-inch half-moons

(Use only the white and light green parts, discard the heavy green tops)

2 cups fresh green beans (stem-end removed, cut beans into thirds)

¼ cauliflower head (large with core removed and cut into spoon-sized florets)

3 button mushrooms, large, cut into quarters

2 cups Russet potatoes, peeled and diced into ½-inch chunks

1 can diced tomatoes in juice (28-ounce can) (San Marzano tomatoes preferred)

2 ears corn, raw (cut the kernels off the cob)

2 teaspoons lemon juice

2 Tablespoons Kosher salt

1½ teaspoons ground black pepper

Preparation Method:

1. In a large soup pot, heat 2 tablespoons EVOO (or 2 Tablespoons reserved chicken fat.)

2. Add 1 diced onion, medium carrot, leek, celery and 1 clove minced garlic.

3. Sautee for 5 minutes, stirring so it doesn't burn.

4. Add green beans, cauliflower, mushrooms – cook another 5 minutes covered.

5. Add reserved chilled chicken broth and potatoes, simmer on medium-low for 15 minutes.

6. Add tomatoes, corn and lemon juice – simmer for additional 10 minutes.

7. Check seasoning - add pepper and salt as needed (or BTB – see Bob's Hint below.)

8. Add pulled chicken meat (cut into roughly ½" chunks).

9. Garnish with fresh parsley.

Bob's Hint: After making broth, instead of adding salt you can use Better Than Bouillon Chicken Base (2 Tablespoons) for more flavor.

This recipe freezes well.

Lentil Soup

Serves 8

Ingredients:

2 cups brown lentils (dried and rinsed clean)

2 Tablespoons Extra Virgin Olive Oil (EVOO)

2 cups onion (diced small)

3 carrots (diced small)

1 Bay leaf, whole

1 sprig fresh thyme

1 Tablespoon all-purpose flour

3 quarts chicken broth (recommend: Bone Broth from Costco)

½ teaspoon Kosher salt

½ teaspoon ground black pepper

1 Russet potato (peeled and cut into ½-inch pieces)

½ pound smoked chicken sausage (sliced in ¼-inch rounds)

1 teaspoon Balsamic vinegar

1 Tablespoon fresh parsley

Preparation Method:

1. In sauce pot, heat EVOO, then add onions and carrots and cook 3 minutes.
2. Add bay leaf, thyme sprig and flour and cook 1 minute.
3. Add rinsed lentils, chicken broth, salt and pepper.
4. Simmer on medium (just before starts to boil) for 30 minutes, stirring occasionally.

5. Add diced potatoes and simmer until potatoes are fully cooked (at least 15 minutes) semi-covered and stirring occasionally.

6. Add smoked sausage.

7. Finish with 1 teaspoon balsamic vinegar.

8. Remove bay leaf and thyme sprig before serving.

9. Garnish with chopped parsley.

Bobby's Marinara Sauce

Ingredients:

4 Tablespoons Extra Virgin Olive Oil (EVOO)

3 cups onions (diced small)

1 ½ cups carrots (diced very small)

2 cloves garlic, minced

2 cans (28-ounce) San Marzano whole tomatoes (crush by hand or rough chop)

1 Tablespoon dried oregano

3 Tablespoons Bruschetta Sweet Basil & Oregano Seasoning (McCormick)

1 teaspoon Kosher salt

2 teaspoons course ground black pepper

4 ounces red wine (Burgundy preferred)

Preparation Method:

1. Add EVOO and onions in heavy-bottom pot and sauté until translucent.
2. Add carrots and continue to sauté for another 5 minutes on medium heat.
3. Add garlic, cook for 1 minute, then add the rest of ingredients, except for red wine.
4. Break tomatoes with mixing spoon to release liquid.
5. Simmer on low heat for 1 hour or until proper consistency. (If sauce gets too thick add a little chicken stock).
6. Add red wine and cook additional 10 minutes.

This sauce is very versatile. To make a Spanish Sauce for

"Spanish Omelet" or a Mexican Sauce, replace "Bruschetta Sweet Basil & Oregano Seasoning" with McCormick's "Taco Seasoning," Chili Powder, and add sliced Jalapeno Peppers from a glass jar.

Bob's Hint: I like this sauce chunky. If preferred smooth, put cooled sauce in a blender until desired consistency. **Don't blend hot!**

Skirt Steak Marinade

<u>Ingredients:</u>

1 pound Skirt Steak, trimmed of excess fat and silverskin

2 Tablespoons vegetable oil

2 Tablespoons orange juice

2 Tablespoons dry mustard

¼ cup pineapple juice

¼ cup soy sauce, low sodium

¼ cup seasoned rice vinegar

1 cup yellow onion, diced small

<u>Preparation Method:</u>

1. Mix above ingredients thoroughly and place in a large Ziplock bag.
2. Marinate 6-12 hours.

Skirt Steak is a very flavorful cut of meat but tends to be tough when eating. The fruit juice in this recipe will tenderize the meat naturally. The meat is best when cooked on BBQ "HOT" for about 2 minutes on each side. When done, the meat should be 125 degrees F for a medium-rare center. When slicing, make sure you cut against the grain. This will also help make the meat more tender and keep it from being stringy.

Bob's Hint: After cooking/grilling, always let meat rest 5-10 minutes before carving.

Bobby and Papa Eddie's Brisket

Serves 6 to 8

Ingredients:

1 3-to-4-pound flat cut brisket (use only the flat or lean cut)

2 ounces vegetable oil

Kosher Salt and Ground Black Pepper (enough to coat brisket)

1 14.8 ounce can diced tomatoes (San Marzano brand preferred)

3 cups onion (cut in half and sliced into thin strips)

3 cups carrots (cut in half length-wise, sliced into ¼- inch half-moons)

1 cup Heinz Chili Sauce 1-½ cup red wine

1-½ cup beef broth

Preparation Method:

1. Preheat oven to 350 degrees F.

2. Use a roasting/braising pan large enough to fit brisket flat on the bottom (do not use a "non-stick" pan.)

3. Add vegetable oil to pan and heat until oil is hot.

4. Coat entire brisket with generous amount of salt and pepper.

5. Sear brisket on both sides until brown (4 minutes per side on medium high), then remove from pan. Add the can of diced tomatoes (with juice), scrape the bits of meat on the bottom of the pan with a mixing spoon and reduce liquid for approximately 3 minutes, until tomatoes are a loose paste consistency.

6. Return brisket to the pan and smear the brisket with

the tomato mixture and cover with Chili Sauce.

7. Place remaining ingredients (onions and carrots) over the top of brisket.

8. Pour 1 cup each wine and beef broth and cover with a tight-fitting lid (can use aluminum foil)

9. Bake in the oven for 2 hours, then check the brisket and add up to ½ cup each of wine and broth if necessary.

10. Cook 2 more hours.

11. Brisket is ready when a meat fork goes in and turns easily, without springing back.

12. Remove the pan from the oven and let rest for 1 hour, uncovered.

13. Remove the tomatoes, onions, and carrots and put them into a separate container.

14. Remove the brisket from the pan and wrap it in tin foil, then wrap in plastic wrap.

15. Put the sauce from the pan in a separate container.

16. Refrigerate all in separate containers overnight.

17. The next day, skim the fat from the sauce.

18. Cut the brisket into ¼-inch slices (slices should be made cross-grain) and place in 10 x 12-inch aluminum pan.

19. Pour the sauce over the meat and add remaining vegetables on top.

20. Cover with aluminum foil and reheat in 350-degree oven for 45 minutes.

When serving, remember Papa Eddie. "I can never remember a time when he wasn't proud of me." That served me well throughout my life! If you use this recipe, you'll feel the same way.

With love, Bobby

Turkey Bolognese

Serves 4

Ingredients:

4 Tablespoons Extra Virgin Olive Oil (EVOO)

1-½ cup onions, diced small

1 cup celery, diced small

1 cup carrots, diced small

2 cloves garlic (crushed and minced)

1 pound ground turkey (dark meat)

4 Tablespoons Bruschetta Sweet Basil & Oregano Seasoning (McCormick)

1 can (28-ounce) San Marzano whole tomatoes (crush by hand or rough chop)

20 Kalamata olives, pitted and cut into half

1 can (4-ounce) sliced mushrooms in water, drained

1 can (4-ounce) green chiles (mild or spicy), drained

10 mini bell peppers, fresh, seeded and diced into ¼-inch pieces

1 teaspoon Kosher salt

1 teaspoon ground black pepper

1 ounces red wine (Burgundy preferred)

Preparation Method:

1. In a Dutch Oven, add EVOO, onions, celery and carrots.

2. Sauté 6-7 minutes, until onions just start to brown.

3. Add garlic and sauté for 1 minute.

4. Add ground turkey and Bruschetta seasoning, and continue sautéing until all turkey is light brown in color (another 6-7 minutes.)

5. Add remaining ingredients (except wine) and bring to a boil.

6. Reduce heat to medium low and simmer for approximately 1 hour or until mixture had tightened to desired consistency.

7. Add wine and continue to simmer for 10 additional minutes.

8. If at any time mixture gets too thick, add small amount of chicken broth.

9. Serve with cooked pasta.

Bob's Hint: Nice to have 2 ounces tequila to drink with ½ lime and ice while making Turkey Bolognese.

Smokey Joe's BBQ Beans

Serves 6-8

Ingredients:

Cooking spray or Crisco

6 slices bacon (6-7 ounces total)

1 onion, small (diced small)

2 cans (15-ounce) Bush's Best Baked Beans (original)

¼ cup Heinz ketchup

1 teaspoon Worcestershire sauce

2 Tablespoons brown sugar

½ teaspoon dry mustard

2 ounces molasses

1 teaspoon Liquid Smoke

1 ounce red wine vinegar

Preparation Method:

1. Preheat oven at 350 degrees and spray baking dish with cooking spray or coat with Crisco.

2. Fry bacon until done but not crisp. Set aside to cool (reserve bacon drippings.)

3. Chop bacon into ½-inch pieces and place in large mixing bowl.

4. Sauté onion in bacon drippings until translucent (5 minutes) and add to mixing bowl.

5. Add ALL remaining ingredients to bowl and gently mix.

6. Pour into prepared baking dish and bake at 350 degrees, uncovered, for 1 hour.

7. The finished beans should be bubbling hot when served.

This can be prepared one or two days before serving. To re-heat from cold, add a small amount of beef or chicken broth to keep beans from scorching.

Bob's Hint: While cooking, listen to Johnny Horton's "Smokey Joe's Bar-B-Que." You can find it on audio streaming services like Spotify or Tidal.

Shrimp Creole

Serves 4

<u>Ingredients:</u>

1 Tablespoons Extra Virgin Olive Oil (EVOO)

2 cloves garlic, minced

2 large onions, diced

2 stalks celery, chopped

8 fresh mini bell peppers, seeded, cut in ¼-inch rings

2 teaspoons Old Bay seasoning

1 can (28-ounce) San Marzano whole tomatoes (crush by hand or rough chop)

1 Tablespoon Worcestershire sauce

2 bay Leaves

1 can (4-ounce) diced Ortega green chiles, drained well

2 bottles (8-ounce) Ocean Clam Juice

2 cans (6 ½ ounce) clams (chopped, in juice)

1 teaspoon Kosher salt

1 teaspoon ground black pepper

24 shrimp (medium) (16-20 per pound), peeled, deveined

2 whole green onions, sliced thin for garnish (white and green parts)

Optional: For a kick, add 2-3 dashes of Louisiana Hot Sauce (Red Rooster or Crystal)

<u>Preparation Method:</u>

1. In a large heavy pot, heat EVOO, garlic, onions, celery, and sliced mini peppers.

2. Cook until soft, about 7 minutes.

3. Stir in Old Bay seasoning.

4. Add tomatoes, Worcestershire, bay leaves, diced green chilies, clam juice, and clams.

5. Season with salt and pepper.

6. Simmer until liquid is reduced by one-half.

7. Place cleaned and deveined shrimp in sauce and cook for about 2-½ minutes. Shrimp will turn bright pink in color when done - don't overcook the shrimp!

8. Serve over cooked rice, and garnish with green onions.

Bob's Hint: Sauce can be done ahead of time (everything up until adding-in the shrimp).

When ready to serve, heat sauce to a boil, then add shrimp and follow preparation method above.

John Sola's Chicken Pot Pie

Serves 8

<u>Ingredients – Chicken Stock Pot Pie Mix:</u>

4 ½ pounds chicken thighs & legs (3 cups cooked chicken meat – shredded or fork-sized)

3 cups chicken bone broth (or favorite chicken stock)

1 cup butter (2 sticks)

6 Tablespoons flour

3 shallots (medium, finely chopped)

2 cups carrots (medium, diced)

1 cup onion (medium, diced)

12 ounces mushrooms, fresh, small (Crimini or Button, quartered)

1 package (10-ounce) frozen peas (thawed)

1 cup heavy cream

3 dashes hot sauce (Tabasco or Cholula)

1 Tablespoon fresh lemon juice

<u>Ingredients – Pastry:</u>

1   package (24-ounce) Puff Pastry (thawed)

2   eggs, beaten (plus 1 Tablespoon water – egg wash) Kosher or Sea Salt / fresh cracked pepper (to taste)

<u>Preparation Method – Chicken Stock Pot Pie Mix:</u>

1. Place all chicken pieces in a 5-quart Dutch oven.

2. Add stock and bring to a boil - immediately reduce to a simmer.

3. Cook chicken until internal temp of 165*F. (15

minutes)

4. Remove chicken and let cool.

5. Strain and skim fat from broth.

6. When chicken is cool enough to handle, pull all the meat from the bones and cut into fork size pieces.

7. Discard bones and skin.

8. Wash Dutch oven for the next step.

9. Melt all the butter in pot on medium heat.

10. Add shallots, onions and carrots and cook for 5 minutes.

11. Add mushrooms and cook 5 more minutes.

12. Add flour and cook 2 minutes forming a paste (Roux). Keep stirring - a light brown color on the bottom of pot is good.

13. Add all the stock and cream. Stir well to get all the Roux incorporated.

14. Raise the heat to medium/high and simmer mix for 15 minutes, stirring to make sure it doesn't stick. (Liquid will reduce slightly.)

15. Add cooked chicken, hot sauce and lemon juice. Cook for 1 minute.

16. Check seasoning - add salt and pepper to taste.

17. Stir in peas - set aside to slightly cool.

Preparation Method - Pastry:

1. Dust a little flour on a very clean counter top.

2. Unfold thawed puff pastry, and with rolling pin, level off to 1/8-inch-thick sheet.

3. Trace round disks using the bowl you're putting the pot pie in to measure.

4. Place cut disks in refrigerator for 20 minutes to chill.

5. Beat 2 eggs with 2 Tablespoons water until well-blended forming an egg wash.

6. Fill 5 to 6 oven-proof bowls (about 5-inch diameter) with pot pie mix – don't go above rim.

7. Brush the rim of each bowl with egg wash to help seal the pastry.

8. Lay pastry disk on top of bowl/filling, pinching edges to seal against the bowl.

9. Brush entire pastry top with egg wash.

10. Cut 3 slits in the top of pie to allow steam to escape.

11. Place pies on cookie sheet to catch any spills.

12. Bake in a 425 F degree oven for 15 minutes, then reduce heat to 350 F degrees for 10 more minutes.

13. Let rest 10 minutes before cutting and serving.

When Mike, Richard, and I developed the concept for The Grill, we wanted to differentiate it from the national steak houses. In addition to the finest Prime steaks, chops, and fresh seafood we wanted to have some comfort food. The obvious choice was Chicken Pot Pie. The Chicken Pot Pie became the number two best-selling item on the lunch menu.

Papa Eddie's Carrot Cake

Serves 16

Cake

Ingredients:

1½ cups sugar

½ cup brown sugar 1½ cups vegetable oil

4 eggs, large

2 cups flour

1 teaspoon baking soda

1 teaspoon salt

1 ¼ teaspoons baking powder

2 teaspoons cinnamon

3 cups carrots (grated, raw)

1 can crushed pineapple (8-3/4 ounces, drained)

1 cup golden raisins (soak in hot water for 15 minutes to plump) strain well

½ cup chopped walnuts

Crisco or Non-stick spray (like Pam)

Preparation Method:

1. In food processor, blend sugar, oil and eggs together (wet ingredients).

2. In stainless steel mixing bowl, mix together flour, baking soda, salt, baking powder and cinnamon (dry ingredients).

3. Combine with egg mixture.

4. Add carrots, pineapple, raisins and walnuts, and

stir with rubber spatula.

5. Turn into 3 greased and floured 9-inch layer pans.

6. Bake at 350° degrees F for 35 to 40 minutes.

7. Perform toothpick test – insert in center, should come out clean, no batter!

8. Cool 15 minutes in pans.

9. Turn out and cool further on wire racks.

Frosting

Ingredients:

½ cup butter (1 stick at room temperature)

1 package (8 ounces) cream cheese, whipped

1 teaspoon vanilla

2 cups powdered sugar (unsifted)

Preparation Method:

1. In food processor, combine butter, cream cheese and vanilla using plastic blade.

2. When blended smooth, add sugar gradually, beating well.

3. Spread cream cheese icing smoothly over top of all three cakes.

4. Place cakes one on top of the other (for 3-layer cake).

5. Spread the rest of the icing around the side of the 3 layers.

6. Decorate by sprinkling with shredded carrots.

Tip: when frosting use rubber spatula. Dip rubber spatula in water to smooth icing.

Bobby says: Enter this cake into any cooking contest and you will be a winner! Just make sure to give Pappa Eddie some credit.

John Sola's Rice Pudding

This Rice Pudding is served at The Grill on the Alley in Beverly Hills

Serves 6-8

Ingredients:

2 quarts whole milk

1 cup Cal-Rose Rice

¾ cup granulated sugar

½ stick butter

1 cinnamon stick

½ teaspoon Kosher salt

1 vanilla bean (preferred) – but can use 1 Tablespoon vanilla extract

2 egg yolks

2 Tablespoons water

¼ pound raisins (soak in hot water for 15 minutes to plump)

¼ cup ground cinnamon

½ cup powdered sugar

Preparation Method:

1. Bring to a boil the milk, rice, sugar, butter, cinnamon stick, salt and vanilla.

2. Reduce heat to medium low and cook for 25 minutes.

3. Blend egg yolks and water together, then add to mixture and simmer for another 10 minutes - stirring often.

4. Remove from pot and transfer to another container.

5. Let cool to room temperature.

6. Mix in raisins, then put in refrigerator until cold (about 2-3 hours.)

7. Combine ground cinnamon and powdered sugar, and sprinkle on top before serving.

Awards & Honors

The Grill on the Alley was inducted into *The Nation's Restaurant News'* Hall of Fame (June 1995).

- *The Nation's Restaurant News* is the top publication in the restaurant industry and is the most prestigious award given to a restaurant.

Awarded the "Spirit of Life Award" From the City of Hope Los Angeles Foodservice/Hospitality Industry for distinguished service to the people of Los Angeles as a Philanthropist and Humanitarian (September 2000).

"Elizabeth Bruns Lifetime Achievement Award" given out by the Los Angeles Chapter of the California Restaurant Association (June 2005).

Past Chairman California Restaurant Association

Past Chairman California Restaurant Association Education Foundation (CRAEF)

Director and past chairman of the Board of Advisors for The Collins College of Hospitality Management at Cal Poly University Pomona

Director for the California Culinary Academy in San Francisco, CA

California Restaurateur of the Year (2006-2007)

Robert Mondavi Wine & Food Award (2006 – Robert & Leslie)

Fred Hayman Visionary Award presented by the Beverly Hills Chamber of Commerce (2019 – Robert & Leslie)

Bob Spivak

At age 7, Bob Spivak was cutting and prepping vegetables in the Los Angeles kitchen of his father Eddie Spivak's Smokey Joe's barbeque restaurants, establishments which inspired two hit songs and a Broadway play. He later managed the food department at Fedco and worked with the owners to develop the Soup 'n Such restaurants. Bob later partnered with Mike Weinstock and Richard Shapiro to open The Grill on the Alley, a traditional American Grill and one of Beverly Hills' most popular restaurants with a reservation list of famous Hollywood Stars and powerbrokers who came for the fine dining experience, the steaks, and the Chicken-Pot-Pie. The Grill was inducted into *The Nation's Restaurant News'* Hall of Fame in 1995.

Bob went on to form Grill Concepts, Inc. and opened Daily Grill, a more casual version of The Grill on the Alley, in 20 cities across the U.S. as well as several gastropubs known as Public School. He later partnered with Chuck Frank and formed Spivak & Frank Restaurants, LLC, to develop restaurant concepts and has worked for Dunkin' Donuts, Baskin-Robbins, and Take A Bau.

Bob is past Chairman of the California Restaurant Association, past chairman of the California Restaurant Association Educational Foundation (CRAEF), has served on the board of the California Culinary Academy and was past chairman of the Board of Advisors for The Collins College of Hospitality Management. In 1965 he was appointed to the California delegation to the United States Commission on Civil Rights and served three years on the commission. He has received many honors and awards, including the California Restaurant Association's Elizabeth Burns Lifetime

Achievement Award and the California Restaurateur of the Year for 2006/2007. Bob and Leslie received the Robert Mondavi Wine & Food Award in 2006.

Bob retired (for the second time) in 2016 and lives in Brentwood, California with his wife Leslie and dog Daily. They have four children: Jason, Elissa, Todd, and Dayna and 10 grandchildren. Bob likes to spend time with their children and grandchildren, cook for family and friends, and travel. He and Leslie take one or two major trips a year.

Laurie Spivak

Laurie Spivak is a researcher, writer, and consultant. She has written case studies and developed curriculum for Masters' and PhD students at the UCLA Luskin School of Public Affairs, as well as articles for a variety of online publications. Laurie holds Masters degrees from UCLA and the London School of Economics, where she was a US-UK Fulbright Scholar. Laurie is Bob's daughter-in-law.